"We're all born with a beautiful mind, but without the owner's manual for operating it! Scott Kiloby's latest book, *Natural Rest for Addiction*, is the owner's manual we're all yearning to possess. Through simple, direct, and flawless instruction, Kiloby shows us how to navigate difficult emotions, obsessive thoughts, and addictive behaviors. And he exquisitely reveals how to experience our natural state of wholeness—which is already present, but so often misunderstood—in which true and lasting healing is present. I deeply appreciate Kiloby's wise counsel that shows how lasting healing and true health can unfold, no matter our circumstances, through simply learning to rest in our natural wholeness."

—**Richard Miller, PhD**, clinical psychologist, president of the Integrative Restoration Institute (www.irest.us), and author of *The iRest Program for Healing PTSD*

"Scott Kiloby has married deep spiritual insight with practical, doable tools to create a truly new paradigm in recovery. Using the Natural Rest method and the Compulsion Inquiry can bring about profound transformation even in addiction, usually one of the most intractable human challenges."

—**Fiona Robertson**, senior facilitator and trainer of Scott Kiloby's Living Inquiries, and author of *The Art of Finding Yourself*

"In *Natural Rest for Addiction*, Scott Kiloby brings his refined practice of present-moment awareness to the healing of addictions and other compulsions, teaching a gentle but deep self-inquiry whose ultimate goal is liberation."

—**Gabor Maté, MD**, author of *In the Realm of Hungry Ghosts*, and cofounder of Compassion4Addiction (www.compassion4addiction.org)

NATURAL REST
for
ADDICTION

**A Radical Approach to Recovery
Through Mindfulness & Awareness**

SCOTT KILOBY

NON-DUALITY PRESS
An Imprint of New Harbinger Publications

Publisher's Note

Distributed in Canada by Raincoast Books

Copyright © 2017 by Scott Kiloby
        Non-Duality Press
        An imprint of New Harbinger Publications, Inc.
        5674 Shattuck Avenue
        Oakland, CA 94609
        www.newharbinger.com

Cover design by Amy Shoup

Acquired by Jess O'Brien

Edited by Susan LaCroix

All Rights Reserved

Library of Congress Cataloging-in-Publication Data on file

19   18   17

10 9 8 7 6 5 4 3 2 1   First Printing

This book is dedicated to my mother, Carolyn.
With tears, love, and gratitude, I wish you the
deepest eternal rest and peace.

Contents

Foreword

What is spiritual awakening? And how is it relevant to recovery from addiction?

There are so many books on the subjects of self-improvement, self-help, spiritual awakening, and addiction recovery available these days. So many methods, practices, programs, teachers, and teachings that often seem so very different, even contradictory. So many people promising us so much, and it can all be so confusing for people who are genuinely open to discovering true peace and rest in their lives.

There are so many questions...

Which method works best?

Can I just stop using my drug of choice without support from others or the help of a method?

How do I know when I'm recovering from addiction?

Is recovery just about being abstinent? Or is it something more than that?

Is spiritual awakening what I need to overcome addiction?

Is spiritual awakening an "event" that happens to some people and not to others?

Is awakening something that can be reached through methods at all?

It can get so exhausting, trying to figure all of this out with the poor little mind! But *Natural Rest for Addiction* clears away this confusion. If you are looking for a way to overcome addiction that is simple, accessible, and practical, yet deeply penetrating, then this book stands out from the crowd.

I have known Scott for many years now. He is a teacher who does not simply regurgitate concepts that he has learned from others. His words have been uniquely forged in the fire of his own pain. He speaks with authenticity and integrity from his own deepest experience, and teaches not by trying to be a teacher, but by being a living example of what he teaches. He is a rare breed—a teacher who actually lives and breathes his own message.

Scott speaks of recovery from addiction through spiritual awakening. But he expresses his message in such a practical, down-to-earth way that at first you may not even realize you're reading a book about spiritual awakening! His words carry deep wisdom, but he avoids all those heavy, esoteric concepts found in the ancient scriptures and traditions. He also doesn't overload you with mountains of intellectual knowledge about the science of addiction, but gently takes you by the proverbial hand and shows you a way out of the insanity of the mind, and its endless seeking for something more in the future. Through clear explanations and piercing inquiries, he shows you that the present moment is always, always the key to recovery. And he shows you how safe it is to dive headfirst into the moment, and to stay there. His method is a truly living meditation that you can take with you into every moment of your life.

Scott points you to the discovery of who you really are, beyond who you think you are—a vast, quiet, non-dual ocean of present-moment awareness that deeply and unconditionally welcomes all thoughts, sensations, and emotions, all energies of life, as they arise and dissolve in you. When you cease identifying as a limited, deficient, and separate "self" looking for freedom and peace in a future moment, you recognize the freedom that exists here and now—the very last place you'd ever think to look!

Make no mistake, this book will challenge your assumptions about addiction and recovery. And it will also challenge many of your deeply held beliefs about yourself and the world around you. Be prepared to let go of some of your cherished concepts about life!

Despite what common sense and conventional wisdom tell us, it is actually incredibly healing to stop running away from present-moment pain and discomfort, and to just sit with those energies as they come up in you, to welcome them as friends that are trying to help you or even awaken you, rather than as enemies that are trying to destroy you. However strange it may sound, much of our suffering comes not directly from our pain and discomfort, but from our attempts to escape that pain and discomfort in the moment.

Most of us attempt to distract ourselves from pain, or numb ourselves to it, or avoid, transcend, or even destroy it. We do this through thinking; through ingesting drugs, alcohol, or other chemicals; through shopping, working, gambling, or sex; through seeking external validation or love; through seeking money, success, self-improvement, or enlightenment; or even through seeking future recovery. As this cycle of seeking plea-sure and avoiding pain takes over, it begins to run our lives. We end up swinging wildly between these polarities, caught in a continuous search for something more, never finding an end to this cycle, often feeling far away from true peace and content-ment and love.

Scott painstakingly points out the futility of always seeking to escape what is. Drawing from his own experience with addiction and years of working with others, he points to resting in presence, allowing ourselves to feel whatever we feel, even if what we feel is deeply uncomfortable, intense, or even painful. He shows us how to allow all thoughts, all feelings, all bodily energies—positive and negative, light and dark—to just be there, as they are, and to relax into the wide-open space that holds them. He points repetitively to this "resting" throughout the book, with good reason. We don't always hear or under-stand this approach the first time round, or even the second or third time. It sometimes takes a degree of repetition for us to see in our own experience the sheer futility of escaping, and how the escaping is the problem, not the solution. To the mind, Scott's approach may seem upside-down or backward, even a little bit crazy. But then, as Scott reminds us, you are not the mind at all.

Some religions and spiritual ideologies promise a future time, perhaps after death, where all discomfort will be swept away. Our parents, out of love, tried to protect us from feeling discomfort in the first place. The entertainment industry turns our attention away from discomfort every day. The advertising industry feeds on our discomfort and dissatisfaction with the way things are. Some self-improvement methods just give us new ways to escape dissatisfaction, thereby making an enemy out of it. Some teachings or methods even tell us that there is something wrong with us if we experience "negative" energies at all!

From all sides we receive the basic message that there is something wrong with us, that we are not okay as we are unless we are feeling 100-percent perfect and comfortable and secure and happy all the time. We are led to believe that we are deficient or broken in some basic way, that we are fallen sinners, that we are psychologically unsound, that we are even beyond repair. We are conditioned to believe we are addicts and always will be. From all sides we get the same message: *you are not good enough*. And so addictive seeking becomes the constant companion of our lives.

Nobody has ever shown us how to be with discomfort, how to welcome it in, how to say *yes* to the uncomfortable energies of life, how to stop identifying with them, so they release naturally and effortlessly. But Scott shows us how. He constantly reminds us that there is nothing wrong with us, and never was. He shows us that, at the most fundamental level, we are deeply okay as we are. At the very core of our being, there is a wholeness that cannot be put into words, an inner silence, a deep stillness that just got a little bit neglected over the years and needs some new friendship. Through his teachings, we come to recognize ourselves as the perfect calm in the midst of the storm of life, the natural rest that never, ever leaves, even when things on the surface do not seem so restful.

I am amazed at Scott's ability to bring the ancient teachings of spiritual awakening down from the mountaintops, onto the streets, into the room that you are in, into your heart and into the deepest, darkest recesses of your intimate personal experience. He fearlessly shines light into addiction's darkest hiding places, and guides you toward an ever-present freedom the likes of which you never imagined possible.

Above all else, this teaching frees you from something that is at the core of all addictions—your addiction to self.

This is a truly wonderful book, and it's likely to reach people who have never before been reached by this kind of work. May you discover the rest that you have always longed for—the rest that you already are. I leave you in Scott's capable, trustworthy, and experienced hands.

—Jeff Foster
Author of *The Deepest Acceptance*
http://www.lifewithoutacentre.com

Preface: My Story

For over twenty years, I lived in addiction.

My addiction progressed from smoking marijuana as a teenager to drinking lots of alcohol and using many drugs, including methamphetamine, opiates, cocaine, and LSD later in life.

Near the end of this dark cycle of using, I was swallowing handfuls of prescription painkillers several times a day. My health was failing. My skin was yellow. The guilt and shame were overwhelming. I hid my addiction from everyone, ashamed of what my life had become.

Through the help of wonderfully supportive friends and family members, I was finally able to quit using drugs and alcohol. Yet, the addictive cycle continued in other ways. I found myself caught in subsequent addictive patterns related to money, food, caffeine, tobacco, relationships, sex, attention or acknowledgment, and seeking self-improvement and enlightenment. I realized, as so many do, that drugs and alcohol were not the problem—"I" was the problem. There was something about me that made life on earth synonymous with the need to escape and avoid.

I searched through many self-help, positive thinking, religious, and spiritual programs. I read tons of books, watched many videos, and followed the works of a long list of teachers. I was hunting for healing but nothing seemed to provide permanent release. I'd make a little progress here and there, in terms of reducing the addictive seeking, but even my desire to end my addiction became an addiction. Through the help of some wise teachers and an intention to look more deeply into my experience, I finally found the key...

Freedom from addiction is already contained in the one place an addict refuses to look—the present moment.

This changed everything!

How did I find that freedom? Well...the short story is this: After reading some books on mindfulness, I began to witness my thoughts rather than indulging them, feel my emotions and sensations without any labels or stories on them, and rest in the present moment as often as possible. This resulted in a gradual but major shift in perception, such that the present moment became the foundation of my life.

A few years before this book was born, I developed the Living Inquiries—you can read about them later in this book. The Inquiries helped me tremendously in finally putting to rest the more deeply held self-esteem issues such as the sense of being unlovable and not good enough. The Inquiries also helped resolve trauma I had experienced in childhood, and carried into adulthood, as a result of being bullied repeatedly by classmates.

I eventually founded a mindfulness training program called the Living Inquiries Community that trains people all over the world in how to use natural rest and the Living Inquiries on all sorts of issues, including addiction, depression, anxiety, obsessive-compulsive disorder (OCD), and trauma. The training program is for those who wish to help others—and themselves also—to go deeper into this work.

Eventually, I began to develop the deeper bodywork that you will encounter in chapter 7. This was the most profound stage of my journey, as deeply held energetic blockages and repressed emotions began to dissolve away, leaving my body feeling very light and transparent. When these blockages dissolved, the last remaining addictions fell away.

During the process of learning, developing, and practicing the tools in this book, I had many subtle and powerful transformational or spiritual experiences, including a profound sense of the oneness of all of life. There were also times when I encountered deep emotional pain, and periods of time where I felt blocked. But all experiences come and go—good and bad. What has remained, and endured, is a deep and abiding peace and acceptance of life as it is. This has provided an amazing capacity to be and love myself, no matter how I show up in any given moment.

For many years, I kept quiet about this treasure, unable to fully articulate it in book form. Because natural rest has to be *experienced* rather than only understood by the mind, it took me a while to find the right words to share it with others. Finally, one day a few years ago, these words came. Actually, they gushed out of me like a heavy downpour of rain in early spring. The result is this book. This book is not a thesis on the science of addiction. It is not the story of my addicted life. It is an instructional book. I've mapped out these tools in great detail to help you with addiction.

Once the book was written, I opened the Kiloby Center for Recovery in Rancho Mirage, California, and the Natural Rest House detox and residential center in Palm Springs, California, with the help of many gracious people. I also became a California Certified Addiction Specialist. The Kiloby Center for Recovery has become a unique laboratory in which I, along with a team of great counselors and facilitators, have taken the tools in this book and expanded them into a very successful addiction treatment program. I am in the process of helping to bring these tools into other programs and facilities across the United States.

Please accept this gift! I invite you to take this book and the tools within it as deeply as you can into your life and watch the transformation happen. You will likely struggle along the way. I did. The struggle is part of the process. But if you stick with it, I believe you will find the treasure I have found and realize that this treasure is contained right here, right now in the present moment—the one place the addicted mind refuses to look.

Freedom from Addiction

Are you constantly looking for the next fix, the next high? Are you always looking for something else, something more?

Does life feel as though it's missing something?

Does it feel like you can't find the complete satisfaction you're seeking, no matter how much you look for it?

...No matter how many drugs you take or drinks you drink?

...No matter how much stuff you buy?

...No matter how much you work?

...No matter how many experiences you have?

...No matter how much love or sex you get?

...No matter how much you gamble or eat?

If you answered *yes* to any of these, you may be suffering from *addiction*.

Addiction is the gaping hole in our lives that can never be filled.

Whether it's a full-blown heroin addiction or an inability to stop scarfing down cookies, addiction has a way of controlling our lives. It sets us on a course of constant, uncontrollable seeking toward the *next* moment.

When addiction is present in our lives, we crave the next moment, and the next, because we seek to avoid any unpleasant, painful feelings and thoughts appearing *now*. These thoughts and feelings are remnants of the past. We unconsciously carry them with us and erroneously believe that the future will somehow set us free. We keep searching for a release from our past emotional and psychological pain as well as any feelings of lack, restlessness, or boredom. In our addiction, there's no such thing as "enough." We just keep seeking, and seeking, and seeking. Yet, *never* finding...

No matter how much we keep seeking a future free of pain and lack, we never find the end of the seeking thread. In our addiction, we may find moments of release or brief periods of satisfaction because we've temporarily quenched our urges, but we never find an ongoing, permanent release from the cycle of avoiding and seeking.

These brief moments inevitably fade because *all* experiences are temporary.

In not finding the lasting freedom we crave, we suffer further, which only causes us to seek into the future more and more. It's a never-ending cycle.

But there is a way you can find unlimited freedom from addiction.

It is called *natural rest*, and you will encounter it in this book.

Natural Rest: Don't Think, Just Do

When we are addicted, we're constantly thinking that the future will give us satisfaction—thinking itself fuels our addiction, and becomes part of it. But the problem is, addiction to thinking can never be released through more thinking. Instead, it only perpetuates the cycle of addiction.

So you won't be able to rely on thinking to find your way into natural rest. Instead, this book will take you on a journey where you can actually *experience* natural rest for yourself.

Natural rest is found in the present moment—a place where we're not emphasizing or obsessing on our thoughts as much, not carrying around so much pain and fear. This rest is "natural" because it's already here for us. It's the felt sense of *presence*.

This book starts with one simple practice: *the practice of resting in the present moment.*

Let's take a moment and experience natural rest.

As you place this book down for a moment, begin to notice your breath.

Take a few long, deep breaths. Stay aware of your breath the whole time. This helps to slow down your thinking for a moment.

As thinking begins to slow down, begin feeling into the aliveness of your inner body. Notice sensations. Feel them without placing labels on them.

Then begin to notice other aspects of your present-moment experience—including sounds, shapes, colors, and smells.

Notice those elements of your experience without placing labels on them.

Rest in that present-moment space for a few seconds.

You have now taken a moment of rest. It may have lasted only a couple of seconds, maybe more. That's perfectly fine. The key is that you tasted it. Experiencing this practice is important before you dig deeper into this book. And continuing to experience natural rest throughout the day, as often as possible, helps you to experience present-moment awareness on a more ongoing and stable basis. This book is all about cultivating the experience of present-moment awareness and letting it infuse every aspect of your life.

Presence: An End to Endless Seeking

Presence is not a belief system.

It's not a program in which you have to convince yourself of certain mental viewpoints. It's not a complicated manual about how to live your life. It's not a code of conduct that you memorize and take with you everywhere you go. It's not a set of affirmations that you have to frequently repeat. It's not dependent on positive thinking strategies.

Presence is much simpler and more immediate than any of this.

Presence is our natural way of being in the here and now without emphasizing our stories as completely true and real. Stories may still arise, but they begin to feel lighter and more transparent once the present moment becomes more predominant for us. This way of being is always and already available in each moment. Once we recognize this, the cycle of addiction can finally begin to relax!

Typically, recovery programs provide only temporary thinking strategies to keep addicts from relapse. Some programs involve taking medications or use other methods and technologies that deal mainly with the *symptoms* of addiction, such as cravings and compulsions, or focus only on certain areas in an addict's life rather than looking at the whole. Those programs have their place. Some people benefit from them.

Other programs speak of a need for spiritual awakening in order to overcome addiction, and in my belief they are right: that's what it takes. But then these same programs may tend to keep us searching addictively toward the future for our awakening, constantly focused on ourselves in a self-centered way. Other programs are based solely on belief systems: "Believe this and your life will change!" But if we don't believe in the tenets of that system or if we begin to seriously question the ideas of that belief system, we may find ourselves at odds with that program. This can place us at risk of continued addiction or relapse. We may then lose the opportunity to find true and lasting recovery from addiction.

The difference with natural rest is that it is based in experience, not in medication, thinking strategies, or belief systems. In natural rest, you are no longer holding back the dam. In some other programs, you get a sense that the individuals involved are holding back the dam of their addictions, as if—at any given moment—the dam could break and they could spiral right back down into the full-blown addictive cycle. I once took my partner to a recovery meeting containing about 150 people. When we left, he said, "The energy in that room was unbearable, as if almost everyone there was right on the brink of relapse." Holding back the dam, or "white-knuckling it," is no way to live. It is not freedom.

As you experience natural rest in your life, you begin to no longer feel as if you are holding back the dam. This is because you have allowed everything to come and go—every sensation, craving, emotion, and thought. You have allowed the dam to break each day, in each moment, while remaining stably present and aware through the whole process. You've allowed the blockages of energy in your body to gradually release, so that they no longer scream for relief through addictive substances and activities.

Presence provides the stability for a deep transformation in how you relate to all experience. It strips away your ability to avoid and escape, and opens the door to facing everything, rather than running from it.

Most addiction-recovery programs are well intentioned, and in aggregate they've helped many people. It is also true that many people do not find long-term recovery in some of the existing programs. The national success rate for alcohol and drug addiction recovery in the United States is approximately 10 to 20 percent. That is very low. It's alarming! Even if people do not relapse using their drug of choice, they often find themselves caught in subsequent addictive patterns, substituting one addiction for another. Instead of booze it's food. Instead of heroin it's alcohol. Instead of gambling it's sex.

Why all this substitution?

Substitution happens because there are facets of the addiction cycle that recovery programs often don't fully or effectively address. These facets include issues like depression, anxiety, and trauma. But perhaps more importantly, these programs don't address the seeker identity itself. The addict is an insatiable seeker—one who addictively looks for satisfaction in the future but never truly finds it. It is the seeking, and the seeker identity of the addict, that renews the addictive cycle.

In natural rest, we see through the seeker identity. This releases the mental and emotional seeking energy within us—the energy that drives all addiction.

Through resting in presence on a repeated basis and using the other tools in this book, we naturally stop addictively seeking the future for our sense of self. As we cease our compulsive looking to the future, this natural, restful presence begins to permeate every part of our lives, providing rest, freedom, and well-being in all the areas where we've been trapped by the cycle of addictive seeking.

Natural rest is authentic spiritual awakening, which is the only thing that can truly uproot addiction.

Presence in the moment holds a profoundly transformative power for us. It eases cravings, anxiety, trauma, depression, and obsession. But most of all, presence has the capacity to dissolve the seeker identity within us, so that we begin to live fully aware of the present moment, allowing everything to be as it is. The present moment becomes our stable and reliable home. Since addiction is all about escaping or avoiding what is, presence becomes an antidote to the constant desire to escape or avoid.

Most of the time, we don't even know *what* we're seeking or *why*. We just know that an uncontrollable urge arises within to look for something else, something more, in the very next moment. The restless mind is our constant companion.

What we're seeking more than anything else is the end of the seeking itself. We're looking for our minds to rest, so we can enjoy life in the present moment.

This book was written to provide the tools to discover that freedom is right here, right now, in the one place we've been overlooking: *this moment!*

Once the seeking falls away, the positive attributes of peace, compassion, love, ease, freedom, and well-being arise naturally. We come to see that these attributes are not things we acquire in time, but inherent attributes of our own restful, present nature.

By now, you may have some obvious, skeptical questions, such as "Can it be this easy? Can the answer to addiction be within me already? Can it really be in the here and now?"

Yes! This is the great news. On the other hand, we're not saying, "You're already free." Such an assertion would be detrimental to anyone already caught up in the energy of seeking because it would give that person a false sense of mental certainty.

Mental certainty about *anything* will never deliver stable, ongoing rest. The certainty of natural rest is *experiential*, so to know directly its transformative power you must come to experience this rest for yourself. Practice is needed for this realization to occur fully in your life.

Although this treasure lies in the natural rest of the present moment, remember: addiction is the constant movement to escape from the present moment and the uncomfortable thoughts and feelings of the past.

You want to deal directly with this movement of escaping so you can shine a light on it, investigate it, and allow it to dissolve into the peace of presence.

How to Use This Book

Natural Rest for Addiction is written for anyone suffering from addiction to anything—not just drugs and alcohol. In this book, I use the word "addiction" in the broadest sense: addiction is the repetitive, compulsive need for and use of anything, including any substance or activity in order to escape uncomfortable or painful thoughts, emotions, and sensations that are arising.

Substances include alcohol, drugs, food, chemicals, or anything else that alters one's mood once it enters the body, creating a desire to use it repeatedly. This includes bingeing.

Activities include gambling, work, sex, surfing the Internet, viewing pornography, seeking self-improvement or spiritual awakening, or anything that results in a compulsion to engage in it repeatedly as a way to escape or avoid.

Addiction includes compulsively emphasizing thought for a sense of self. For this reason, virtually all humans are addicts, regardless of whether they've experienced the habitual tendency to use addictive substances.

Addiction is often accompanied by the sense of having little to no control over the desire to use the substance or engage in the activity. Addiction often negatively affects many areas of our lives, including our mental, emotional, and physical health; relationships; families; and work, as well as wider aspects of society, such as our health care and legal systems.

Natural rest is not a method based on self-improvement. It's not aimed at improving the sense of self through striving toward the future. Instead, recovery is based on seeing through the ego or sense of self that lives in our thoughts of past and future. In this way of recovery, seeking a more improved sense of self over time is considered just *another* form of addictive seeking.

Although resting in presence is the central practice of this book, it contains other tools, including a technique called "stop, notice, and repeat," which you'll learn in chapter 3.

Far and away the most powerful supporting tools for the practice of the Natural Rest way of recovery are a series of contemplative exercises called *the Living Inquiries*. Resting in presence gives us freedom in the moment; practicing the Living Inquiries uproots long-held stories that keep us reaching for substances and activities for relief. You will find the Living Inquiries in chapter 6.

You will see the term *energies* defined differently in various places in this book. In the broadest sense, the term includes anything that comes and goes temporarily within our awareness, such as thoughts, emotions, sensations, sights, sounds, smells, tastes, states, experiences, cravings, and behaviors. But for the purposes of our journey through this book—and to keep it simple—consider energies to be three things: words, pictures, and bodily energy.

Our experience in any given moment can be broken down into words, pictures, and bodily energy. For example, when we think of a lemon, we may see the mental image of a lemon, hear the word "lemon" streaming through the mind, and feel an energy or sensation in our mouths or stomachs. This is how we experience a lemon, through the combination of words, pictures, and energy. Without this combination, we cannot internalize the experience of the lemon, know what to do with it, or even know what it is. This is how we experience everything, including ourselves, other people, and every other object in our reality.

Whenever you see the term *thoughts* in the book, know that it is referring to the words and mental pictures that arise and fall in your mind. And, although the terms *emotions* and *sensations* are used throughout the book to describe what we feel in the body, notice that emotions and sensations are just bodily energy when they aren't being labeled. Breaking our experience down to these simple components (words, pictures, and bodily energy) makes this book easier to read and makes the Living Inquiries in chapter 6 easier to do.

Don't worry if you do not completely understand this discussion of how these three elements make up our experience. It will become clearer as you read this book and begin the practices in it.

This book contains many short paragraphs separated by spaces. These short paragraphs are invitations for you to deeply experience the words themselves and to look into your own direct experience of the restful presence to which the words point.

Take a moment of rest between each paragraph. Notice how your mind is trying to make meaning and create narratives about yourself, others, and life. By watching these thoughts, and letting them dissolve away one by one, you begin to rest in the present moment more and more. This can be uncomfortable and unfamiliar at first. We are so conditioned to rely on our minds for everything. But allowing these thoughts to dissolve is how we begin to experience a much deeper peace and acceptance in our lives.

The invitation to read this book is an ongoing invitation to experience the natural rest of the moment. If this book helps you, keep it nearby so you can refer to it as a reminder to rest in presence as often as possible.

This book is not about the intellect. The intellect is a practical tool available to us. We continue using the intellect in our lives. But the wisdom and clarity available in natural rest come from a deeper source. This wisdom and clarity are available to all humans through experientially resting in presence as often as possible.

Although many insights can arise in the mind through resting in presence, the clarity of natural rest doesn't come from agreeing or disagreeing with whatever's said here. If you find yourself arguing with the words of this book, it may be because you're frustrated by an inability to see where the words are pointing. Seek support from someone who has direct experience with finding recovery through natural rest.

Another thing that may be frustrating in reading this book is the sheer repetition of some of the main instructions (for example, the instruction to "rest" or "allow all energies to be as they are"). If you find yourself frustrated in this way, it may be that you are trying to read the book to feed the intellect, looking for more information on each page, or reading the book as if it is a story unfolding before your eyes.

This book is not designed to fill your mind with more ideas, tell a story, or provide complicated theories of addiction to learn or memorize. The repetition of these instructions is deliberately placed in the book as a constant reminder to experience presence for yourself. This is why taking time between paragraphs to rest and look to where the words are pointing is so vital. Avoid reading the book nonstop from beginning to end, as you would read other books. Instead, just read a little bit every morning or evening, or throughout the day, taking time in between to rest and experience the freedom to which the words are pointing.

Natural rest is different from other recovery programs. It's an unlearning—revealing that life is a mystery that can never be fully understood, only lived. In this recognition, we rely less on thoughts for our well-being. We come to know our well-being in presence instead.

Some will not be attracted to this way of recovery. They may be more interested in continuing to seek the future. This book remains available if that search ever becomes exhausting.

Chapter 1 ("Natural Rest") is a basic guide for experiencing presence on a repeated basis throughout each day. The chapter contains some of the essential practices in this book. It may be helpful to return to it often.

The other chapters deal with topics such as cravings, obsession, self-centeredness, relationships, seeing through stories of self-deficiency or lack, dissolving body contractions, misconceptions and traps, and freedom.

Presence as a Way to Recover

Before you dig into this book, it's important that I explain a little about the context. In this book, natural rest is referred to as a "way of recovery" for a reason. Seeking toward the future is one of the hallmarks of addiction. A recovery program that has us chasing the future has at least the possibility of feeding the addictive cycle within us.

If the key to freedom from addiction is found through presence, then how can presence be reached via a way? Doesn't the word "way" itself imply a time-bound method—that is, the movement from now to some point in the future?

To answer that, we have to take a closer look at who we are as humans. We're used to thinking of ourselves as stories involving a past, present, and future. All our lives, we've been conditioned to think of the future as the key to unlocking whatever it is we're seeking. So at first, it's only natural that we approach this way of recovery within that same, familiar way of thinking.

Yet, through the Natural Rest way, we eventually wake up and out of this conditioning—out of the false belief that we must somehow seek the future to find our sense of fulfillment or well-being. As we rest in presence, we come to see that we're already whole and complete in the here and now. We find less need to identify with thoughts of the past and future. As this happens, our stories become less important to us. And, as our stories become less important, our sense of living in time gradually dissolves, leaving only the peace and freedom of timeless presence.

Some may begin to practice this way and discover instantaneous presence. They're ready to live there! Because it happened so quickly, they might not experience resting in presence as a way or method at all.

For most of us, however, a complete recognition of presence doesn't happen in one fleeting instant or even overnight. For that reason, this book was created as a way to ease you into restful presence, gradually. Although this approach may give the impression that you're moving toward the realization of presence in the future, in actuality the story of needing the future is falling away.

How long does it take for you to recognize presence in all areas of your life? It will take exactly how long it takes. So relax and enjoy the ride! And always, always, always trust your own experience.

NOT A SUBSTITUTE FOR REHAB

If you're currently using alcohol, drugs, or other chemicals, we strongly encourage you to seek professional help if you cannot quit on your own. This way of recovery is *not* a substitute for medical attention and it's *not* a detoxification program. Detoxification under the supervision of health care professionals may be necessary before you begin the Natural Rest way. You should always consult a physician or addiction specialist before and during your participation in any program—including this one—especially if you are addicted to substances that may have life-threatening withdrawal effects. In some cases, medication is needed before you can effectively focus on the practices in this book.

I am a cofounder of the Kiloby Center for Recovery. The Center is a supportive atmosphere where I and my trained facilitators work with people every day using the tools in this book. Some who read this book may need the kind of ongoing support and care offered at the Center, especially those who need detox, those who would benefit from a more comprehensive program, those who have difficulty quitting on their own, or those suffering from more extreme forms of addiction, anxiety, trauma, or depression. Trauma can be especially overwhelming and difficult to deal with on your own. If you read this book and continue to struggle, please contact the Center at http://www.kilobycenter.com.

The practices and inquiries in this book should also not be treated as a complete substitute for some other treatment or recovery program or method that's working positively for you. This way of recovery can powerfully complement what you already have. Please ease into the practices and inquiries here to see if they work for you, before abandoning other methods or recovery programs that have been helpful.

Although this book focuses on interior awareness as a key to recovery, other important measures should not be discarded or ignored. For example, an emphasis on good physical health, nutrition, exercise, and sleep is vitally important to recovery.

For those who are ready, natural rest can be a major key to true and lasting freedom from the addictive cycle.

Because the tools in this book are highly experiential, I want to offer you a gift that I believe will help tremendously in bringing this work into your everyday life. Because you purchased this book, you now have free access to the entire library of audio offered by the Kiloby Center. These are the tools our clients use each day at the Center.

Go to http://www.naturalrestforaddiction.com. Click on the "Resources" tab at the top. On the drop down menu, click on the option "Members Only"; this will take you to a page called "Scholarship and Aftercare Program." Click on "Log In," and when you're prompted, type in "kilobycenter" as the username and "rest" as the password.

CHAPTER 1

Natural Rest

Natural rest essentially refers to being present or living more in the moment. But how do we do that? Our minds and bodies seem so wrapped up in the past and future. In order to get a clearer sense of what natural rest is all about, let's break it up into three parts, which can be seen as three practices:

1. Rest includes taking moments repeatedly throughout the day for thought-free presence.

2. Rest includes noticing thoughts (words and pictures in the mind) come and go, without judging, analyzing, or commenting on them.

3. Rest also includes bringing attention directly to bodily energies (emotions and sensations) and allowing them to be as they are, without trying to change, neutralize, or get rid of them.

The remainder of this chapter breaks down these practices one by one.

Brief Moments of Rest

How do we experience brief moments of thought-free presence? Below, I've provided some portals.

Three to Five Seconds

Relax for three to five seconds right now and simply be, *without any conceptual labels* for what's presently happening. Stop thinking for one moment! Right now! It's easier to start with just three to five seconds at first. As you practice these brief moments repeatedly throughout the day, it gets easier and the moments become naturally longer. It's like riding a bicycle: At first you may be able to stay on the bike only for a short time, before you fall over. But after practice, you are able to stay on the bike and ride for much longer periods of time, until eventually riding a bicycle is second nature.

Awareness of Breath

If you find it difficult to stop thinking for a few seconds, focus your awareness on your breath. Breathe through your nostrils, not your mouth. Take a few deep, long breaths, keeping your attention on the breath the whole time. Watch your breath move all the way down the body into the stomach area, then watch it move all the way up and out of your nostrils. Focusing on the breath helps to stop or slow down the mind.

Noticing Thought Followed by Thought-Free Rest

Another portal into thought-free rest is the noticing of thought. Notice that you have the capacity to be aware of thought. Remember, thoughts are either mental pictures you see in the mind or words you hear or see in the mind. Notice the words or pictures that are currently appearing. Look directly and gently at the thoughts and watch them fade away naturally on their own. Notice them from a quiet, witnessing space, without judging, analyzing, or commenting on them. As they fade completely, simply rest in the thought-free space that remains.

Inner Body Awareness

Inner body awareness can also be an effective way to experience a brief moment of thought-free rest. Bring your attention into the felt-sense of peace or stillness within your chest or stomach area. As you bring attention there, you will likely notice some sensation, but you should also notice that, as attention is drawn away from the mind, there is a subtle sense of peace or stillness in the inner body. Rest your attention in that area for a few seconds. As you experience the peace or stillness within the body, expand your attention to notice that peace or stillness all around the body and everywhere else.

It doesn't matter which portal you use; the key is to notice what a brief moment of rest feels and looks like. What's here, in this moment, when you aren't labeling it? Nothing can be said. Nothing needs to be known. The mind is quiet for a brief moment. For a few seconds, past and future thoughts aren't arising.

Addictive seeking arises through emphasizing past and future thoughts. When you're taking a brief moment of rest, you're already completely free of the story of past and future—for that moment at least. It's important to gain this insight, even if you realize it for only a few seconds. That moment of insight is revealing that your addiction resides mainly in your mind, although there is certainly a bodily component to it, as we will discuss later.

The key is to find one of the portals to thought-free rest that works for you and to use it as often as possible throughout the day.

How often is often? Well…as often as you can. As often as possible. If you can only take a brief moment every fifteen minutes, then start there. If you can take it more often—such as every five minutes, every minute, or even every thirty seconds—then start there. You may even want to wear a wristwatch or use a timer to remind you to rest repeatedly. The more you repeat this practice, the more often you will be able to rest in thought-free presence automatically, naturally, and effortlessly, with less time between those moments of rest.

When you stop thinking for a bit, you tap into the experience of awareness. Awareness isn't any thought, emotion, craving, obsession, state, experience, sight, sound, smell, taste, or other sensation that appears and disappears. It's not any of these things. These things are all temporary.

Different stories have come and gone within this presence throughout your life. The story coming through when you were ten years old is different than the story coming through at age twenty, thirty, and so on. But the presence in which those stories come and go *never* changes. It's always here. I'm using "presence" and "awareness" synonymously.

It's the same presence, no matter what's coming through. This is an important insight. To gain this insight, you have to experience these brief moments of rest repeatedly. You have to actually notice that each time you take a brief moment, that open, spacious awareness is available. It's the same awareness each time you take a brief moment.

In taking brief moments of resting in presence, we come to see for ourselves that this presence lies at the foundation of our experience, always. It is fundamental to our experience. It provides a stability and well-being in our lives that temporary words, pictures, and bodily energies cannot provide.

Presence is *that which is aware of* all of these temporary words, pictures, and energies coming and going.

Each time we rest in still, quiet, thought-free presence throughout the day, we experience the relaxed, open view of the present moment. Instead of narrowly focusing on a story in the mind or a single object, person, or event, we take in the fullness of the present moment without thought and allow our focus to be wide open and relaxed. We notice space in front of, behind, between, within, and all around everything we see. Experiencing this spaciousness is very beneficial. It helps reduce stress, anxiety, and addictive thinking.

Noticing Words and Pictures

Remember, at the top of the chapter I said that rest includes three components. The second component is noticing thoughts.

Our thoughts (in the form of words and pictures) are coming and going within the space of the present moment, and these thoughts are merely telling a self-centered story. They aren't happening in the pure, vivid reality of the present moment. They are not like tables, houses, and mountains. They don't have the same kind of dense physical existence. They are more temporary in nature, ethereal and transparent. You can't touch them. Words and pictures are projections of the mind. I can't see your thoughts and you can't see mine.

This self-centered story, which we experience through these words and pictures projected from or within the mind, has been trying to escape the present moment. It's a time-bound story. In the story, we're always rehashing or reexperiencing the past and fantasizing about a better future, or fearing the future. We continuously overlook the present-moment, where life *actually* happens.

Each of these words and pictures temporarily appears and disappears in the unchanging, stable space of present-moment awareness.

Our stories are constantly changing. When we emphasize the content of thoughts instead of resting as the silent witness of them, the temporary nature of thought leaves us feeling unstable about who we are. This feeling makes us seek the future to find a sense of self. Yet we never find a complete version of ourselves this way. We only find more seeking toward the future.

How do we begin to notice these words and pictures? Look now and notice that the story of who you think you are appears through words and pictures. Focus *very gently* on the current set of words or pictures that are arising. Slow the current words or pictures down, and just observe them quietly, again, without judging, analyzing, or commenting on them. When you observe words and pictures this way, you are allowing them to be what they are—temporary arisings. In this allowing, you notice that each thought falls away on its own, dissolving into the space of presence. When it falls away, take a brief moment of resting without thoughts.

It can help to peripherally notice the space around a set of words or a picture you are looking at. For example, look at a mental image of a tomato. As you are looking directly at it, don't turn attention away from the image. But notice peripherally the space around the image and even in front of and behind it. Let the image just float freely in that space. Notice how the image begins to dissolve into that space. Opening your attention peripherally to the space around a mental picture allows you to relax the clinging, resistance, or attachment to it. This, in turn, allows it to dissolve more easily. The dissolving of words and pictures happens on its own. No need to try and force it to happen. Forcing it can add more resistance. Instead, just let it be as it is, witnessing it gently, even allowing it, *as if you want it to stay there.* Wanting it to stay there can actually reverse the clinging, resistance, or attachment. Wanting it to stay is like loving it exactly as it is. Loving anything that arises has a deeply transformative effect. It allows everything to dissolve gently back into the space of present-moment awareness.

Words are a little different. Certainly you can visualize words you are hearing and see them written out in the mind. If so, look at them directly and notice the peripheral space around them. Watch them dissolve into that space, just as a picture dissolves. But some people hear words in their mind, more than they see them spelled out. If this is your experience, then just

25

hear them without judging, analyzing, or commenting on them. Treat them as a meaningless sound you are hearing. Notice the space or silence around them. Let the sound dissolve naturally into the quiet space of presence. Again, no need to try and force the dissolving of words you hear in the mind. Gentle noticing and allowing is enough. They will dissolve away on their own time, in their own way. The more gently you notice things, the better.

Picking up this practice throughout the day around the story-based words and pictures that you experience allows you to experience presence. Watching these words and pictures come and go, and then dissolve back into presence, provides a mental and emotional stability that's not available when we are indulging in our stories constantly.

At first you may notice that you are only able to witness the words and pictures. You may have difficulty detecting the awareness or presence in which they are coming and going. This is why it helps to rest in the thought-free presence that remains when any words or pictures dissolve. Sooner or later you will start to notice that this presence is always here and always available whether there are words and pictures arising or whether there are no thoughts happening at all.

Bringing Attention to Bodily Energies

Let's move now to the third component of natural rest—bringing direct attention to bodily energies such as emotions and sensations. This practice is critical to overcoming addiction, perhaps more important than anything else.

Addiction is all about the desire to escape or avoid uncomfortable or painful emotions or sensations that we are experiencing in the present moment. Resisting these bodily energies as they arise in the moment merely keeps them around. As they stay around, and we are unable to cope with them, we may feel compelled to reach for our addictive substances and activities as a way to escape or avoid. Therefore, bringing attention directly to these energies and allowing them to be as they are is an antidote to addiction.

But how do you do that? The first step is to acknowledge that you are feeling something. We tend to acknowledge emotions and sensations first through the mind. We might think, *I'm angry* or *I'm afraid of what might happen*, or we may simply notice that something is bothering us, without being able to articulate it. But we cannot feel emotions or sensations through thinking. These thoughts are narratives or labels for how we feel. They are not the actual energies themselves. For example, if you have the thought *I have a stomachache*, that thought is a label for something that is actually happening in your body, apart from the thought. In order to actually feel or experience the stomachache directly, you would have to bring attention down into the stomach area and feel it without thoughts on it.

The same is true for all emotions and sensations. Once you acknowledge that you feel something or have been triggered by someone or some event, bring attention very gently to the body where you feel the actual emotion or sensation. Attention should be so gentle that it is almost like you are loving and accepting the energy exactly as it is, without any desire to change, neutralize, or get rid of it. In order to do this, you may first have to notice any thoughts or stories you have about the emotion or sensation, and witness the thoughts or stories until they fade away into presence. Don't push the thoughts away; just witness them gently as described above. Witnessing allows them to fade away on their own. As they fade away, it becomes easier to drop attention down into and around the emotion or sensation.

Once your attention is there, feel into the sensation or emotion and become aware of the peripheral space around it at the same time. Let the emotion or sensation just hang there in the open space, without trying to change, neutralize, or get rid of it. It is common to want to change, neutralize, or get rid of it. Just notice any tendency to want to do these things. These movements are resistance itself. It's like trying to fight what is happening, instead of loving and allowing.

If you find that the resistance to the energy remains, it can be helpful to say directly to the energy, "Thank you for arising, I love you; stay as long as you like." I call this the *Thank You phrase*. You will see it repeated several times in this book. Saying this phrase may seem counterintuitive or even uncomfortable at first. But it works for many people, so do try it. Resistance means that on some level in your experience (conscious or unconscious), you do not want this energy to be arising, you do not love it, and you would like it to go away. Using this phrase helps to reverse that resistance.

Sometimes you have to rest with (in other words, allow) the resistance to the emotion or sensation first, before you can truly be with the emotion or sensation directly. Witness and allow resistance until it fades naturally into presence. Use the Thank You phrase (above) on the resistance if needed. What's left is the actual energy of the emotion or sensation. Once you have no thoughts on an emotion or sensation and very little or no resistance to it, the emotion or sensation tends to fade away on its own. Stay with it, quietly, until it fades. It may take a while.

Most emotions and sensations fade away on their own once we are not adding thoughts or resistance to them anymore. Again, do not try and force an emotion or sensation to go away. This will just add more resistance. Love it, welcome it, allow it!

Do this practice all day, throughout the day, whenever you feel anything. It may be difficult at first. But as you do it more and more, it becomes more natural and automatic. You are essentially changing the habit of suffering. Instead of thinking about how you feel, you are just feeling it quietly until it fades naturally. Instead of resisting how you feel by trying to change, neutralize, or get rid of it, you are allowing emotions and sensations to be as they are in the open space of presence. This is acceptance. Acceptance is the antidote to addiction.

Now that you have learned the natural rest practice broken down into three components, the key is to practice, to experience natural rest throughout the day, all day, as often as possible.

Keep the following in mind always when doing the practices mentioned above: *we give power to words, pictures, and bodily energies by turning awareness away from them; we diminish their power by turning toward them and remaining aware of them until they fade naturally.* That one simple understanding, if turned into a daily practice, is highly transformative.

There's Nothing to Chase

As you start the practices above, it is important to have some context around natural rest and how it helps with addiction. In addiction, we live with a story of deficiency, a sense of needing something else, something more in the future. It always feels like something is missing in life. This story of deficiency is a set of words that repeatedly say, "I'm not good enough," "I'm not there yet," or "There's something wrong with me." This story arises with painful emotions or sensations of restlessness or boredom.

In order to escape these feelings and sensations, we consciously or unconsciously indulge thoughts about the future. Thoughts arise that tell us we need to seek a reprieve or a pleasurable high in the next moment in order to cover up boredom, restlessness, or painful feelings that we're experiencing in the body.

When we emphasize these thoughts, instead of resting in presence, they lead us into the cycle of seeking the future. We never find permanent relief this way. We only find a temporary fix, which leads us to chase the reprieve or pleasurable high, again and again.

But a fix found in the next moment is only temporary. The story of deficiency and its corresponding emotions and sensations return once the fix wears off, leading us back into the cycle of seeking a fix in the next moment.

We're like dogs chasing our own tails.

Restful presence is experienced to be complete just as it is. The more we practice it, the more we realize and experience this completeness. This is when addiction begins to fall away. All of your addictions may not fall away all at once. You may see them fall away one at a time. The key is to just stick to the practices.

This Isn't About the Future

It is difficult for some people to truly grasp the notion that presence is available always in the here and now, yet recovery from addictions is a gradual process. It seems paradoxical. But the process is not really about reaching a later point in the future when you are finally free of all addictions. Don't set yourself up in that way or you will be constantly chasing the future, which is the very definition of addiction. This is about settling more and more into the present moment, where you experience the ability to naturally let go of one addiction at a time, as you experience presence as being more and more foundational in your life.

Quite simply, the more presence infuses your life, the more complete you feel in the moment and the less likely you are to want to use addictive substances and activities to escape or avoid uncomfortable or painful words, pictures, and bodily energies. This is the irony of this kind of work. We simply aren't always ready to put down every addiction at once. We have to become ready to examine and release each addiction.

At the Kiloby Center, we first help people get off drugs and alcohol using these practices. Then clients begin to deal with other addictions over time (such as sugar, caffeine, and tobacco), when they become ready to rest and allow all the words, pictures, and energies connected to these secondary addictions to fall away. Although presence is always available as a resource in the here and now, the falling away of addictions happens gradually for most people.

Don't look for quick results. Don't look for future results. Just pick up and use the practices in this book regularly. Start by dropping one addictive substance or activity. Then focus on others when you are ready.

Recovery in the Natural Rest way is not about addictively seeking a future point where you become a perfect person free of all addictions. It is a natural resting in the present moment, allowing everything to come and go, so that you become less and less hooked into the words, pictures, and energies that compel you toward addictive substances and activities.

Natural Rest Is Our Home

In picking up the practices in this chapter, we come to realize that our home is in the natural rest of presence.

What do we mean when we say "presence is our home"? This "home" is not something we find, like an object, a place, a state, or even a single experience. It is not a thought either. It is also not a future moment, as stated above. It is the recognition that all words, pictures, and bodily energies come and go, and what remains cannot be understood. It cannot be grasped. It can only be experienced. It is rest itself. We call it "home" because, as we rest more and more, this rest feels natural and available always. All of these words are merely ways to describe the experiential seeing that no matter what energies are coming through, they simply pass once we notice them and do not follow them. Presence is freedom from believing we are our thoughts and the other temporary energies that come and go.

Nothing that comes and goes temporarily can be what we really are.

As we notice the rest of the present moment as being always available, life is experienced as peaceful, free, open, and uncontrived. We find less or no need to apply effort to mentally label or control our experience, others, the world, or ourselves. We are naturally open to any thoughts, emotions, or other energies that may appear and then disappear.

We see that these thoughts have no power to destroy or divide the natural rest of presence. They're temporary arisings. That's all.

In the natural rest of presence, we're not at war with thoughts. We don't need to be. They have their place. In fact, we continue to use thinking for practical purposes, such as driving a car, talking to a friend, working, or buying groceries. Practical thoughts are still useful. It's the rest from constantly indulging in our personal stories that provides the key to freedom from addiction.

In the beginning, we may experience rest as a temporary state that we visit repeatedly throughout the day or a practice that we employ over and over. But through repeatedly resting in and as present-moment awareness, we discover natural rest as the very nature of our being. It settles into our experience fully and finally. This is not about practicing for the rest of your life. At some point, natural rest becomes an experiential recognition that the present moment is the foundation of our experience. We then just live from that presence.

If presence doesn't feel like your home, it's okay. For now, just pick up the practices. Use them when you are lying, sitting, standing, or moving, when things are going well in your life and when things are not going well, when you are working and at home, in the morning, throughout the day and at night. Use them during moments of excessive thinking or in moments where there is very little thinking happening. Use them when you feel good and when you feel bad.

You may read this and wonder how you can realize that presence is available when things are not going well in life or when you feel bad. But remember, presence is not about changing how we feel. It is not about trying to feel better. Addiction is the cycle of always trying to feel better or escape negativity. Presence is about being aware of and allowing whatever is happening—even pain and fear.

You may also wonder why you would want to use these practices when you feel good. But all feelings are temporary—even positive ones. Allow those to be as they are and to dissolve like everything else. Realize that your home is presence itself. When you look only for positive feelings, you will be let down. Everything comes and goes.

In recognizing awareness as always present and available, it begins to permeate every aspect of our lives, every experience, and everything that comes and goes. This is why we call it "natural." It begins to no longer feel like a decision we're making or a practice we're employing. It becomes our home. We can rely on it completely.

This must be experienced. It cannot be grasped through thinking.

The Pond Metaphor

The following metaphor may give you a taste of what it means to say that presence becomes the foundation of our lives, no matter what is happening in any given moment.

Imagine a pond in your mind's eye. The pond is completely still on a summer day. It's totally at rest in its natural state.

Like the pond, the natural rest of presence is quiet and still.

Like ripples across the surface of the pond, words, pictures, and bodily energies appear and disappear within quiet, still, restful presence. Some of those ripples are small movements, and some are big disturbances. We suffer and remain addicted because we believe the ripples are what we are, instead of recognizing the restful underlying presence as what we are.

Rather than recognizing the natural restfulness of presence (the pond), we're looking for a permanent sense of self where it can't be found (in the ever-changing temporary ripples).

We've been identifying with these temporary words, pictures, and energies, while chasing pleasure and avoiding pain. This keeps us constantly seeking. This seeking becomes our identity.

We've been operating on the assumption that seeking is necessary. We've been assuming that it takes excessive thought to simply live and be. We've been assuming that it takes worry, anxiety, and stress in order to live.

None of these things are essential to life. Presence is the only thing that's essential because presence is always here.

Resting in present awareness throughout the day is the simplest, most effective thing we can do for ourselves as addicts.

The simple practice of resting in presence reveals that seeking, worrying, and excessive thinking aren't necessary at all. Restful presence is already free of everything because it allows everything to come and go, like the ripples.

Just as each ripple across the pond is inseparable from the pond but never truly disturbs the stillness of the pond itself, we see that each of the words, pictures, and bodily energies we experience is inseparable from presence and never truly disturbs the stillness of presence itself.

This inseparability is important in seeing that each ripple is a movement of the pond itself. In this seeing, we don't try to push any ripple away. We aren't trying to get rid of the words, pictures, and energies that move through our restful presence.

Everything is allowed—every ripple, no matter how small or big, how pleasurable or painful.

No ripple is closer or more essential to the pond than any other ripple. Each ripple is equally wet and equally "of the pond." The pond is always there, no matter what ripple is moving across its surface.

Similarly, no words, pictures, or energies are closer or more essential to presence (to what we are) than any other words, pictures, or energies. All can be equally allowed, equally allowed to come and go, without fighting or trying to change any of it. Even when we try and fight or change something that is happening, that too can be allowed, as just another ripple. Each is an equal movement of presence. Presence is always here, no matter what's moving through. Coming to know this through direct experience has incredible transformative power.

Key Points

As you begin to practice natural rest, this brief review will help you stay focused on the main points:

Rest in thought-free presence repeatedly throughout the day. Throughout the day, as often as possible, take brief moments of rest without thoughts (in other words, without words and mental pictures). Use one or more of the portals presented at the beginning of this chapter.

Notice words and pictures coming and going. Even when words and pictures are appearing and you cannot rest without thoughts, you can rest as the awareness that notices and allows them to come and go freely. Notice the peripheral space around each thought. Let each thought fade away naturally into that space.

Bring direct attention to bodily energies and allow them to be as they are. Throughout the day, whenever you feel anything in the body, bring attention directly to the sensation or emotion, feel and allow it to be as it is—without placing any words or pictures on it. Notice and allow any resistance to the emotion or sensation. This allows bodily energies to change or dissolve more easily. When bringing attention to an energy, notice the peripheral space around it. Let the energy be until it dissolves naturally into that space.

Again, keep the following in mind always when doing these practices: *we give power to words, pictures, and bodily energies by turning awareness away from them; we diminish their power by turning toward them and remaining aware of them until they fade naturally.*

CHAPTER 2

Cravings

Let's start right away with dealing with cravings, since they predominate our experience when we are addicted to anything.

Cravings are words, pictures, and energies that come and go temporarily within restful presence. Nothing more! Because of their temporary nature, they initially have no power to harm us. They only gain power when they arise—unseen. To say that a craving arises unseen means we don't see it as a temporary thought that carries with it a corresponding sensation in the body.

Whenever we notice that a craving is only a thought (words or a picture) with a sensation, it becomes easier to rest, witness, and allow it all to come and go.

When a Craving Arises First as Bodily Energy

Sometimes a craving arises first as a sensation in the body, and you aren't aware of any words or pictures arising with it. You just know you crave something, but can't quite pinpoint why.

Imagine a soapy bubble rising out of a hot bath. This is how cravings sometimes appear—subtly, spontaneously, and involuntarily. They're movements of anxious energy that arise from the restful space within the body.

Remember what I said in chapter 1: We give power to what arises in our bodies and minds by turning away; we diminish the power of words, pictures, and energies by turning toward them and remaining aware of them until they naturally dissolve.

Whenever we fail to notice these sensations the moment they appear in the body or soon after, they can gain power and momentum. They often fuel a rapid firing of thoughts related to substances or activities we crave (such as gambling, sweets, or a drug of choice).

If you can notice the sensation first, before it fuels the rapid firing of thoughts, then very gently bring attention into the sensation and notice the peripheral space around it at the same time. Rest and allow the sensation to slowly burn up into the space around it. It may be helpful to notice and allow any resistance to the energy first, before bringing attention to the craving energy itself. The Thank You phrase can be helpful. Say to the energy, "Thank you for arising. I love you. Stay as long as you like." This can help relax the resistance so that the craving energy can dissolve more easily. It is natural to want the craving to go away, but the key is to allow it, welcome it, love it.

To feel a craving energy arising in the body doesn't mean you should label it. Don't call it "good" or "bad" or even "a craving." If those or any other labels arise, witness them and watch them fade away. There's nothing to mentally analyze or rationalize about the energy. Remember, words and pictures are merely symbols of the energy. They are not the energy itself. The key is to bring attention to the energy itself.

To feel a craving as energy itself means to feel it without words and pictures on it. Subtle cravings gain momentum when we don't let the sensation arise and fall freely without words and pictures on it.

The experience of thoughts being stuck to sensations is called the *Velcro Effect*. Resting and feeling into the sensation without words and pictures on it undoes the Velcro Effect. It separates the words and pictures from the sensation so that the sensation can float freely by itself in presence until it dissolves naturally. Remember, no force or effort should be applied.

Whenever we experience a craving energy in the body, all sorts of thoughts can arise, including thoughts about wanting to use our favorite drug, thoughts about wanting the craving to go away, or even thoughts that judge, analyze, or comment on the craving.

But it doesn't matter what thought arises, just witness and let it pass. Emphasizing the thought *I want this to go away*, or any other thought, can subtly keep the sensation around.

Each time a thought comes and goes, take a moment to rest in presence. Then, again, bring your attention to the space of the inner body. Feel the sensation again without words and pictures on it, and notice again the peripheral space around it, allowing the sensation to dissolve naturally into presence.

When a Craving Arises First as Words or Pictures

Sometimes a craving arises first as words heard in the mind, such as *I'd really like a beer*, or as a subtle, quickly flashing image, such as a mental picture of a mug of beer. I call these quickly flashing images "ghost images" because they seem to materialize very quickly out of nowhere and then disappear very quickly.

The key is to pick up the practices in this chapter so that you get better and better at spotting these words and pictures in the moment they arise.

If a craving arises as a set of words or a picture, just observe it, as taught in chapter 1, letting it dissolve naturally. If necessary, take a deeeeeeeeep breath and then relax. For a moment, once the thought has dissolved, just be, without any thought. That's a short moment of rest, as described in chapter 1. While in that short moment of rest, bring attention to any sensation (without words or pictures on it) and allow it to be in the peripheral space until it dissolves.

If you start to experience a succession of thoughts, witness each thought come and go until the thoughts have dissolved away. Witness and allow them to come and go without judging, analyzing, or commenting on them, just as you would notice a flock of birds flying past you. When they fly by, one by one, you don't try to grasp at them. You just quietly watch. Do the same with all thoughts related to the craving.

Then bring attention to the energy, noticing the peripheral space around the energy at the same time. Eventually the energy will burn out completely in that space and, when it does, you should experience a reduction or elimination of cravings thoughts.

Don't Wait for Cravings to Appear

Throughout the day, it's important to rest repeatedly in the present moment, instead of waiting for a craving to appear. Rest in moments even when no cravings arise.

In this way of recovery, we don't think of resting as a "remedy for cravings." Natural rest isn't another "fix." In our addictive cycle, we're always looking for the next quick fix.

In the Natural Rest way, *we don't treat recovery as a fix.*

Cravings arise and fall in presence. That's all they do. They come and they go, leaving no trace. They have no other power.

By resting in presence repeatedly throughout the day, we're better able to notice cravings as soon as they arise within the body, *before* they begin fueling addictive and obsessive thoughts about the future.

When we treat presence as a quick fix, we're back in the addictive cycle, looking for temporary relief. When we treat resting in presence as a shift in our identity, we free ourselves from the addictive cycle, permanently. For more on this identity shift, see chapter 4 ("Self-Centeredness") and chapter 6 "The Living Inquiries").

Key Points

Reviewing the following list will help remind you of the key points in dealing with cravings:

Notice body cravings. If a craving first appears as bodily energy only, gently bring attention directly to the energy, while noticing the peripheral space around it. Allow the sensation to dissolve into that space naturally. Love it, welcome it! Use the Thank You phrase if necessary. If it doesn't dissolve, this usually means there are words or pictures "velcroed" to it. Witness and allow those words and pictures to dissolve, then return to resting with the energy.

Notice thought cravings. When a craving first appears as a thought (a set of words or a picture), observe the thought from awareness, letting it dissolve away naturally, without force or effort. Then check into the body for any accompanying sensation. If there is a sensation there, gently allow it to be, while noticing the peripheral space around it. Allow it to dissolve on its own into that space.

Observe successive or rapid firing of thoughts. When we don't observe thoughts and sensations around a craving as soon as they arise, they can turn into a successive or rapid firing of thoughts about wanting to use. In that case, observe the successive thoughts as you would observe a flock of birds flying by, one by one, until they are mostly gone. Then bring attention into the bodily energy and the space around it, allowing it to dissolve into that space.

Don't wait for cravings to appear. It is best not to use these practices only when cravings are appearing. Pick up the practices in chapters 1 and 2 and do them each day, throughout the day. This builds up the muscle of awareness, so to speak, so that you are better able to see and rest with these cravings thoughts and energies as soon as they arise.

CHAPTER 3

Obsession

In chapter 2, I discussed cravings. I stated that cravings can turn into a successive or rapid firing of thoughts and sensations when we aren't aware of them and don't allow them to be as they are as soon as they arise. In this chapter, our focus is obsession. Think of obsession as a very intense craving energy that seems to overtake the body and mind in an unconscious way. It's what we experience when the successive or rapid firing of cravings thoughts overwhelms us, which puts us at a much higher risk of picking up addictive substances and activities.

You can think of cravings and obsessions as existing on a continuum. Cravings can appear in increasing intensity from mild to moderate until they cross a certain threshold of intensity. At that point, we can call them obsessions. Science tells us that cravings are accompanied by anxiety because both come mainly from the midbrain, rather than the part of the brain that engages in rational decision making. The farther you get toward obsession on the continuum, the higher the anxiety. It's important to understand, therefore, that it is difficult to rationalize yourself out of obsession. The anxiety level is too high. Instead we want to focus on how presence can become an antidote to obsession. I provide a method later in this chapter to help with the cravings and anxiety that are inherent in obsession.

Let's start with a basic definition of obsession. For purposes of this book, we define "obsession" as *persistent, intense, unconscious energy in the body accompanied by a continuous, involuntary preoccupation with thought that cannot be removed by logic or reasoning.*

That's a wordy definition. But it's important to speak to all of the elements of obsession so that we know what's happening to us in those moments of obsession, why our old ways of dealing with obsession haven't totally worked, and how restful presence frees this obsessive energy.

Persistent, Intense, and Unconscious

Obsession has a persistent intensity to it that takes it above mild to moderate cravings. Obsession is like being completely overtaken by intense mental and emotional energy.

Obsession is a raging storm within the body and mind with its own self-sustaining power and momentum. It seems to be driven toward a purpose, which is to escape into an addictive substance or activity. It's seeking the future. There is high anxiety in it.

"Unconsciousness" is similar to the notion of "seeing red" when one is angry. If you ask someone after a moment of intense anger to relate what actually happened in that moment, she won't likely be able to describe clearly what happened within her mind and body. The anger was unconscious in that moment, which means it was unseen. In the moment it arose, there was no awareness of the anger.

Similarly, in obsessive moments, whenever they first appear, both the thoughts and the bodily energies are not seen by awareness. This unconsciousness is the fuel for obsession. It's like a small spark that starts a massive fire. When the spark remains unseen, it grows and grows. Obsession can continue only as long as the thoughts and energies remain unseen. We'll talk more about this later.

Energy in the Body

Sticking to the definition above, obsession isn't just thought based. Our bodies are very active in moments of obsession. Heat, tension, vibration, anxiety, fear, and other energies rise up in the body whenever we're obsessing about our addictive substance or activity. Our throats may close. Our chests may tighten. Our stomachs may clinch.

Without knowing what's actually happening within our bodies, we tend to oversimplify obsession, believing it's just a "thought problem." Remember, it's the Velcro Effect that lies at the heart of addiction. Thoughts arise and feel stuck to these sensations of heat, tension, vibration, anxiety, fear, and other energies in the body.

The key to releasing obsession is found through resting in presence, so that the Velcro Effect is undone.

By treating it only as a thought problem, we erroneously believe we can appeal to logic and reasoning (more thoughts) to free ourselves from obsession. This is a vicious, nonproductive cycle in which the thought-based personal will is only trying to overcome itself. This cycle ignores what's really happening within the body.

Continuous, Involuntary Preoccupation with Thought

There's certainly a strong element of thought in obsession, and the thought feels involuntary, as if we're at its mercy.

This preoccupation with thought cannot be removed by logic or reasoning. Remember, intense craving or obsession comes from the midbrain. Obsession essentially shuts down the part of our brain that is logical. Our previous promises to ourselves to "never use again" fall away in these moments. The obsessive thoughts run the show.

It's difficult, if not impossible, to think our way out of obsession. It's like being caught in a raging storm and then believing we can reason with the storm and tell it to calm down. The futility of this becomes more apparent as we begin to rest in the present moment.

Freedom from Obsession

It's important to not wait until cravings reach the point of obsession. Remember, the invitation here is to pick up the practices and use them each day, throughout the day. Don't think of presence as a remedy, a fix, or an antidote that you apply only when full-blown obsession is happening.

Despite the fact that this chapter will give you a plan for dealing with moments of obsession (see "Stop, Notice, Repeat," below), we want to rest in presence throughout the day, not just when obsession is happening.

Obsession is such a powerful storm that waiting for those moments to practice natural rest often results in frustration.

We walk away thinking, *Natural rest didn't help me get rid of my obsession!* This is a misunderstanding of the invitation here.

By resting repeatedly and by being aware of all energies, including happy thoughts, slight irritations, and mild to moderate cravings (see chapter 2) whenever they arise, rest feels more available in intense moments of obsession.

Rest is always available because it's presence itself. Trying to rest for the first time when an obsession has already taken us over is like waiting to walk to the store only after the slight sprinkle of rain outside turns into a downpour. Walk now, whether there's sunshine or a slight sprinkle.

Stop, Notice, and Repeat

If you do find yourself caught in obsession, think: *stop, notice, and repeat.* This is a simple way to explain what it means to apply the tools in this book to obsession. This method helps not only with obsession but also with anxiety attacks and other afflictive states. "Stop, notice, and repeat" is a lot like what you learned in chapter 2 regarding cravings. I have put it into method form here to help you simplify and remember the tools when obsession is taking you over. Because obsession has a way of overwhelming us, the simpler the better.

1. **Stop.** As soon as you recognize obsession happening in the body and mind, stop for one moment. Get quiet.

Stopping alone is not enough because the mental and emotional energy of obsession often has a tremendous, involuntary force that likes to start again immediately after stopping. This is why it's important to notice and repeat.

2. **Notice.** Notice includes both noticing thought and noticing bodily energy during obsession.

   Noticing Thought As soon as you stop, notice whatever thought is appearing within the mind. This thought is the involuntary preoccupation we talked about in our obsession definition. Noticing the thought makes it conscious or seen. Remember: *Unconsciousness is the fuel for obsession.* Simply noticing a thought interrupts it for a brief moment.

   At this point, it's important not to try and think yourself out of obsession. Remember that this preoccupation with thought *cannot be removed by logic or reasoning.* Thinking merely adds more thoughts to a thought stream that's already highly energetic.

   Remember that you cannot reason with a storm. Noticing thought is an important opportunity during obsession. For the first time, there's the capacity to see that the awareness that sees the thought is already at rest.

   Watch the current thought, whatever it is, until it fades away. Rest with the thought, which means allow it to be exactly as it is without trying to do anything with it. Add no additional thoughts for a few seconds.

If you experience a rapid succession of thoughts, witness them as I discussed in chapter 2, like a flock of birds going by one by one. Rest with the entire succession of thoughts, which means allow them to come and go freely as you observe them without placing any meaning on them. The key is to observe thoughts gently and stay with them, without judging, analyzing, or commenting on them.

Noticing Bodily Energy   Whenever you get even a short break from the rapid succession of thoughts, begin to bring attention into the sensation in your body, while noticing the peripheral space around it. Because obsession has such force with it, don't expect all the thoughts to quiet. Just wait for a break in the succession of them, then move to the energy.

Notice any heat, tension, vibration, anxiety, fear, or other energies appearing in the body. There's no need to mentally label, rationalize, or analyze the energies or why they're there.

Remember, you can't reason with a storm. Just notice the raw energy itself, before the mind labels it. This makes these energies conscious or seen. As long as the energies remain unseen, they fuel obsessive thoughts. Let the energy be as it is, without words or pictures, as best you can. Experiencing the bodily energy, by itself, without words or pictures, undoes the Velcro Effect. Notice the peripheral space around the energy, as discussed in chapter 2. Allow the sensation to dissolve naturally. If it doesn't dissolve, that means the mind is still active in the obsession. If so, go back to noticing thoughts coming and going until they dissolve, and then come back to resting and allowing the bodily energy.

3. **Repeat.** Repeat the stop and notice steps over and over as often as possible during a strong obsession until the obsession begins to subside. Even when you do stop and notice for a brief moment, obsession often has such a strong pull that it starts right back up. Suddenly, you find yourself taken by the storm once more. Just stop, again. Notice thought and emotion. Repeat.

"STOP, NOTICE, AND REPEAT" IN PRACTICE

Imagine you're a gambling addict and you've managed to go a month without gambling. One day, you start having small cravings to gamble.

Having already taken up the practice of resting in the present moment, you find it easy to notice the craving as soon as it arises or shortly after.

In noticing a craving, rest in the present moment, keeping your attention on the inner body. With your body and mind relaxed and your awareness alert to the space of the inner body and mind, you notice anytime your mind wanders back into wanting to gamble. This alone may release the energy of craving so it doesn't turn into obsession.

If the cravings start to intensify and you find yourself obsessing, bring in the "stop, notice, and repeat" method. Go to a quiet place if you can.

Notice the thoughts about gambling. Noticing interrupts the power of the thought stream. Watch all the different pictures about gambling and notice all the words about it. Let them all come and go freely like the flock of birds going by.

Bring attention to the bodily energy and the space around it. Let the intense bodily energy that's driving the obsessive thoughts be as it is. No need for any force or will. Just let it be. Allow it to run its course without trying to manipulate it, modify it, or do anything else with it. Don't put a conceptual label on the energy. Imagine the emotion or other bodily energy filling up the room completely, as if your body no longer has a boundary around it and can no longer contain the energy. Let the energy expand fully into the space within you as well as into the space of the entire room. That's the peripheral space that I've discussed many times. Allow the energy to burn up in that space.

If the obsessive thoughts start again—stop, notice, and repeat over and over. Do this again and again until the obsession subsides. The key is infinite patience when it comes to this method. Continue resting with and observing all thoughts and bodily energy until they come to rest. Be patient. Don't try to force the obsession to stop. That will only add fuel to the fire.

Key Points

Whenever obsession arises, use the "stop, notice, and repeat" method:

1. **Stop.** Stop what you are doing. Get quiet.

2. **Notice.** First notice any thoughts. Observe them from awareness. Let them be as they are. Watch each one fade away, one by one. Then move attention to the energy in the body, noticing the peripheral space around the energy. Rest and allow the energy to be. If thoughts arise again, notice them and return back to the body. Eventually the energy in the body should burn out.

3. **Repeat.** Repeat steps 1 and 2 until the obsession subsides.

CHAPTER 4

Self-Centeredness

Addiction is about much more than just cravings for substances and activities. It is tied directly to identity. As addicts, we don't know who we are. We live in an ongoing identity crisis and we're barely aware of it.

During the course of a lifetime, our identities change often. We go from child to friend, to spouse or partner, to employee, to addict, to recovering addict, to sick person, to dying person. None of these labels are our real identity.

They're nothing more than temporary concepts.

Seeking is based on a desire to find a solid and permanent sense of one's self in time.

We keep looking to the future in hopes that we'll find out who or what we are. We keep looking for that next label, material thing, relationship, fix, or awakening. The ego-based story is trying to survive. It's constantly looking for something.

Yet, we never find the answer. There is no stability in this constant game of seeking. The most we ever find is another label with which to identify or another temporary fix.

Natural rest is about solving this identity crisis once and for all.

Through picking up the practices in this book, a stability and transparency of body and mind is revealed. The energies of thought, emotion, and sensation come to rest more easily or arise less. That's the stability. This does not occur by making stability a future goal. This stability arises in the present moment through following the tools in this book. We actually come to realize our true identity as the unchanging, stable presence that underlies everything that is coming and going temporarily.

Aren't all thoughts temporary?

Thoughts are words and pictures that temporarily appear and disappear within presence.

How can you be a temporary word or picture?

Words and pictures tell a story of past and future. Past words and pictures contain the sense of "who I am." Future words and pictures contain the sense of "who I am going to become." These thoughts are all temporary. They arise in a series. The fact that they arise one after another in a series doesn't make them truer. They're still only fleeting concepts that come and go.

Every word and picture that appears within our self-centered stories is appearing to a selfless presence that sees the word or picture. This presence is what we really are, not any of the words and pictures.

Through identification with words and pictures that make up a story, we're seeking to fulfill a self that's illusory, a self that's being created by the activity of thinking itself.

Identification with words and pictures makes us feel separate from one another and from the universe. So we go looking for wholeness in the future. Yet all we find are more words and pictures—more thinking—which just makes us feel more separate. This leads us to look again for wholeness in the future.

We're constantly looking for ourselves.

This is the cycle of seeking. It's our addiction.

It may not be obvious now, but addiction is more than just a compulsion to use or engage in certain substances and activities in order to feel better. It's based in a deeper misconception about who and what we are.

The Endless Cycle of Seeking

Addicts are like hamsters spinning 'round and 'round on wheels inside their cages. We're constantly seeking something more. This constant seeking keeps us imprisoned inside a loop that keeps repeating itself. The loop is made of words and pictures.

We live with a sense of lack or deficiency, a sense that something's missing. The words and pictures keep telling us we're not good enough or aren't there yet. We keep seeking our freedom in the future, but we never find it. We only find more words and pictures that tell us the same story, leading us to seek over and over into the future.

We never fully resolve who we are or what we really want through seeking the future. In not finding real freedom through seeking, our stories feel incomplete. This incompletion is the sense of lack or deficiency. This is a self-perpetuating cycle.

We may find moments here and there when we feel complete or satisfied, but we never reach that permanent state of freedom, peace, and contentment that provides an end to the seeking itself.

Like the hamster, we just keep running.

We keep escaping the present moment. We keep following the wheel of time as if it's real, not seeing that time is only thought.

The time-bound story of self is only a series of words and pictures. This story is designed to feel incomplete.

In this story, we're looking for anything that fills the sense of lack that is our constant companion.

Lack is our constant companion for only one reason: we continue fueling the belief that our freedom resides in the future, in the next moment, the next fix.

Do you see the vicious cycle of seeking? It's the *very thought* that the future holds our fulfillment that makes the present moment feel as if it's lacking. (You may want to read that again.)

This one critical insight can change everything. Each time a thought or sensation arises that tells us this moment is lacking something, we can make the decision to rest in presence and simply observe the thought or sensation coming and going.

The self that we find in words and pictures can't reach fulfillment. It's not supposed to. That's not its real goal. Its only real goal is to keep chasing an illusory future. Like the hamster on the wheel, all of its energy is spent running, never reaching complete resolution, only continuing to suffer.

We need look no further than our own addictive backgrounds to see this is the case. We have all the evidence we need to make a decision to try another way.

When the thought arises that says some future moment contains our freedom, we simply notice it come and go, and rest in presence. This is the key! We find that the contentment we've been seeking is already here. We've been continuously overlooking the obvious freedom of presence.

This is the most important thing we can do for ourselves as addicts. We stop telling the lie that the future is the key. We make resting in presence the top priority in our lives. This decision frees us from the cycle of seeking.

What Are You Seeking?

Ask yourself this question (it's the most important one you can ask in recovery):

What am I seeking?

You may respond that you're seeking to feel better, have fun, or escape boredom, or to find happiness, freedom, love, peace, good health, material success, or something else—even recovery.

But what are you *really* seeking? Look more closely. If you felt better, you'd actually be experiencing *the end of seeking to feel better*. If you found peace, you'd be experiencing *the end of seeking peace*. If you made lots of money, you'd be experiencing *the end of seeking money*. If you found recovery, *you'd actually be experiencing the end of seeking recovery*.

What we're really seeking is *the end of seeking itself.*

We erroneously believe that the end of addictive seeking can be found within the time-bound, thought-based story of self. Let's take a closer look at why the end of seeking cannot be found in that story.

The Self-Center

In this way of recovery, we call the thought-based story of self that lives in time the *self-center.* Calling it a self-center helps us understand what it is and what it does. This understanding helps us see why restful presence is the key to the end of addictive seeking.

The self-center is a set of thoughts moving through time—from past, through the present, and into the future. This story of "me," by its very nature, places the self at the center of life.

The story of past includes our name, history, and thoughts about ourselves, including our childhood and background, successes, and failures. These are all words and mental pictures. When someone asks, "Who are you?" we're likely to answer by referencing thoughts from the past.

But are you a story?

Are you a set of words and pictures appearing within the mind? What does a story of the past have to do with right now? Isn't this moment where life really is?

We normally emphasize either positive or negative thoughts from the past for a sense of self. The thoughts from the past that we emphasize determine how the present moment looks and feels.

If one refers to himself as a victim, for example, he perceives the present moment through the veil of thoughts from his past story of being a victim. This story is a negative conceptual lens and carries negative emotional energy with it.

When a victim looks at the present moment, his eyes reveal a world full of people and circumstances that aren't treating him fairly. His heart is lonely, sad, and angry.

A victim seeks others who will make this story of being a victim seem true. These others buy into his illusion of being a victim. They feed it. They may play the role of perpetrator, or they may just enable him to continue telling the story that he's a victim. This solidifies his sense that he really is a victim.

It's a self-perpetuating story. It's all unconscious. A victim doesn't realize he's doing this. He really believes that life is unfair to him. He believes he really is a victim.

The victim story is unreal. It's only a set of thoughts.

A victim is no different than any other story of self. Every story of self unfolds this way, regardless of the content of the story.

Past thoughts and emotions are carried over into the present moment. They repeat themselves in the future.

Even if one refers to herself in a positive way—something like "spiritual person"—she perceives the present moment through that lens. Her eyes reveal a world in which she believes she's special and others aren't as spiritual as she is.

Although this may be a more positive story, with warm and fuzzy feelings to go with it, it's still only a story. Neither the positive nor the negative stories we tell about ourselves are absolutely true. They're just stories. And all stories, whether positive or negative, make us feel separate from each other. That sense of separateness keeps us seeking out wholeness in the future.

These stories cannot provide the deep and permanent freedom, peace, and contentment that relieve us from the cycle of addiction.

By their very nature, stories are unstable.

In the course of a week, for example, we experience a wide range of ups and downs in our stories. One morning we might feel on top of the world. By the afternoon we may feel really angry because of what a loved one said or did.

The next day we may feel fine. But that night we may experience great anxiety over something coming up later in the week, like a doctor's exam or a work presentation.

In these stories, we identify with whatever thoughts and emotions happen to be appearing at the time. The thoughts and emotions feel stuck together. That's the Velcro Effect. And that's how identification with a self-center happens. It's no wonder we've been reaching for addictive substances and activities to make us feel better. In our stories, we're at the mercy of whatever arises. And, whenever we identify with thoughts and emotions, we're at the mercy of the Velcro Effect.

This way of living offers no stability. As addicts, we tend to avoid the negative feelings and chase after the positive feelings. We often reach for our favorite addictive substance or activity to cover up the negative emotions. The stories, therefore, just perpetuate the cycle of seeking the future. We're seeking some later moment that's free of these negative feelings.

We often feel a need to rehash past negative situations and fixate on our reactions to those situations. Unconsciously, we're trying to protect ourselves from experiencing pain again, when and if similar future situations arise.

This need to self-protect keeps us feeling separate from others. We withdraw emotionally. We play it safe, refusing to be vulnerable and open to life. This mechanism of self-protection obscures the nonattached, nondefensive love available in presence.

We act from memories about whom we are rather than from the total freedom of presence. We often try to predict and plan how we're going to act in some future situation, instead of living in the moment and responding from the heart, from an authentic, uncontrived way of being.

When we carry past labels about ourselves into the present moment, these labels color our present view. They limit what we see and do.

These labels limit our creativity. They keep us focused on ourselves. When we're concerned mainly for ourselves, we can't see a present situation the way it really is. We can't see from someone else's perspective. We can't see the big picture. As a result, true creative action that benefits everyone isn't as available to us.

In these stories, we're more concerned with being special and separate from others than with simply being present with others and with what's happening now.

Separation causes us to feel isolated from one another. Isolation is dangerous for us. In isolation, we're cut off from those who can support us in recovery. It's easier, in isolation, to entertain thoughts of relapse and to act out on those thoughts.

We're neither as good as we think we are nor as bad as we think we are. We're neither positive nor negative concepts. All concepts, positive and negative, appear and disappear within presence.

The Problem with Temporary Fixes

Because we don't know who or what we really are, and we are experiencing an ongoing identity crisis, it is only natural that we would reach toward addictive substances and activities to medicate the pain or escape from our story. But, in doing so, we are operating under the false assumption that a temporary, pleasurable fix can give us the relief we're really seeking.

We can certainly satisfy the sense of deficiency within us *temporarily* in this way. But temporary pleasures cannot provide deep, lasting relief from seeking. In fact, they perpetuate more seeking.

Each time we temporarily satisfy an urge to feel better, we falsely believe our contentment comes from the addictive substance or activity itself. The mind associates relief from seeking with the substance or activity.

Then we're off and running on the hamster wheel, seeking more temporary fixes.

Through resting repeatedly in presence, we start to see what's really happening.

Our contentment doesn't come from the substance or the activity.

When we temporarily satisfy an urge by indulging in an addictive substance or activity, *we're experiencing a brief rest from the seeking toward that addictive substance or activity.*

This is an important insight. We must discover this for ourselves. This *rest from seeking itself* is what we're really seeking. True contentment is not temporary.

Repeatedly resting in the present moment provides deep, lasting relief from the cycle of seeking.

We've been trying to avoid the pain of our past or re-create pleasurable past moments. We've been seeking the future to feel better.

We've been returning again and again to temporary fixes. We've been returning to drugs, food, work, shopping, gambling, or some other addictive substance and activity.

Temporary fixes will never resolve a lifetime of seeking.

Temporary fixes are tiny pit stops along the endless path of seeking the future.

This chase exhausts us. It often has a detrimental effect on our health and relationships.

Temporary substances and activities are only symptoms of our real addiction. We're really addicted to thought. We're addicted to incessantly thinking about ourselves, including where we've been and where we're going. This thinking is based on a present sense of deficiency. But instead of looking at the story of deficiency and seeing it as just words and pictures, we believe it. And deficiency, because it's accompanied by painful or uncomfortable feelings, makes us reach for more temporary fixes.

So how do we end this identity crisis? How do we see that these stories are not what or who we really are? And finally, how do we end addiction? You've already been given many of the tools in the previous chapters. Are you practicing them all day, throughout the day, or are you just reading this book from end to end? In chapter 6, you will learn the Unfindable Inquiry, which is a great tool for dealing with this identity crisis effectively. But it's important for you to learn and diligently use the practices discussed in the earlier chapters before you begin using the Unfindable and other inquiries in chapter 6.

Key Points

Here's a review of the key points from this chapter:

Addiction is an identity crisis. It's not just about the addictive substances or activities we use. Addiction arises from the sense of deficiency and separation we experience in our lives. We experience deficiency and separation through false stories we tell ourselves. These stories are based in past and future. We use addictive substances and activities to medicate, escape, or cover up the pain of these stories.

We identify with our stories. In these stories, we identify with whatever thoughts, emotions, and sensations happen to be appearing in any given moment. The thoughts (words and pictures) feel stuck, or velcroed, to bodily energies (emotions and sensations). That's the Velcro Effect. And that's how identification with a self-center happens.

Practicing rest dissolves self-centered stories. Dissolving these stories happens through diligently practicing the tools in this book and allowing presence to become the foundation of our experience, rather than these stories. Refer back to chapter 1 for essential practices around resting; noticing words, pictures, and energies; and feeling bodily energies directly, without words and pictures on them. The Living Inquiries in chapter 6 (namely the Unfindable Inquiry) can help tremendously.

CHAPTER 5

Relationship

Before you move forward in this book, it's important to discuss relationship and how it plays a key role in identity as well as in addiction and recovery from addiction.

Relationship in this book is defined very broadly. It includes not only your relationships with people or animals, but also your relationship to inanimate objects and everything else in the world.

Whenever you interact with any person or animal, you are in relationship. But you are also in relationship with absolutely everything else that you encounter in life, and each relationship ties directly into who you are and how you live your life. Each time you reach for an addictive substance or activity, you are in relationship with that substance or activity. For example, some smokers say that, when they cannot experience real intimacy with other people, smoking becomes a way to experience intimacy with the cigarette.

You are in relationship with the people you know; the house, city, and nation in which you live; the political party to which you belong; the book you have in your hand right now;

your addictive substance or activity; your past and future; your feelings—literally everything.

Your relationships to people and objects play a central role in how you define yourself and live your life. Virtually everyone and everything in the world is mirroring back, to one degree or another, who you are and how you think and feel about yourself.

Understanding the critical role that relationship plays in your life will help you see the value of the Living Inquiries in the next chapter, will help you gain insight into the identity crisis discussed in the last chapter, and will help you overcome addiction.

Human Relationships

Human relationships can be incredibly challenging for those who find themselves in the cycle of addiction. In our addiction and self-centered behavior, we may have left behind a string of damaged relationships with people who no longer trust us.

We may have used people for personal gain. We may have even stolen from loved ones, or physically or mentally abused others.

We may have placed ourselves in situations in which we were victimized or abused by others.

We may find, even in recovery, a desire to isolate ourselves from others. When we're disconnected from others, loneliness and self-pity can take over. We may find ourselves in conflict with others. When conflict is prominent in our lives, we carry around anger and resentment.

When these negative feelings dominate our relationships, we may find ourselves wanting to resort to addictive substances or activities to cover up or escape the feelings.

But most of all, human relationship is the mechanism by which we mentally define who we are. I know I am an author because you are the reader reading my book. You know that you are a mother or father because of your relationship to your children, and so on and so forth. These are all stories, of course, but the stories seem true because others in the world seem to constantly mirror back to us that these stories are who we really are. And we buy into it, lock, stock, and barrel.

Relationship is also the way in which we develop certain deficiency stories about ourselves. For example, you may feel not good enough precisely because of the dynamic between you and your father. You may feel unlovable as a result of failed relationships with past girlfriends or boyfriends. You may feel inadequate because your boss doesn't seem to appreciate you. You may have developed the desire to help people because helping is what allowed you to receive love from your family at an early age (and when you aren't in a position to help, you may feel invalid or unacknowledged).

The Unfindable Inquiry in the next chapter helps us to see through these false deficiency stories. But even before we learn this inquiry, we can begin to use the practices already discussed in this book to see more clearly and let go of some of the stories that keep us locked into self-centeredness.

Bringing Natural Rest into Relationships

In our relationships, we're often operating from self-centeredness. Old patterns repeat themselves in each relationship.

We try to protect, defend, and bolster a self-image. We erroneously believe our thoughts about others are absolutely true. We want to be right and make others wrong.

We desire that our wants and needs be met first, above others.

We may find ourselves locked in a pattern of using, controlling, and manipulating other people or being used, controlled, and manipulated by others.

We may find ourselves feeling deficient or hurt when triggered by others or when others seem to mirror back that we aren't good enough.

Regardless of what arises in any given moment in human relationship, the key is to rest, notice thoughts, and feel emotions directly as I have discussed throughout this book.

Each time we respond in a relationship from this self-centered story, we solidify a sense of division in the relationship. It's me versus you, instead of "we."

By resting in presence and noticing and allowing the words, pictures, and energies to arise consciously in presence as we relate to other people, we see that the self-center we're trying to protect, defend, and bolster in relationship is merely a set of passing mental images. It's merely thought. And the feelings are just feelings. By allowing it all, relationships are easier to navigate. It's also easier to respond from compassion and love rather than fear, defense, or attack.

To understand and gain insight into how this works, imagine yourself sitting and talking to someone you find challenging. Imagine not being aware of your thoughts or feelings as they are arising. Notice then that you might automatically defend yourself, attack or judge the other person, or tune out. You are trying to avoid the pain or discomfort you are feeling in the presence of this other person.

Avoidance doesn't work. It's also painful.

Now imagine the same scenario, but this time you are resting in presence as you relate to this person. You are bringing attention to whatever you are feeling and allowing it to be in the open space of presence. You are noticing thoughts come and go that are all about defense, attack, or judgment. You let them all come and go and return to a sense of presence, creating the space for the other person to be who they are. From this space of presence, a different way of responding naturally arises. You are able to hear the person better. When you respond verbally, you find yourself not needing to defend, attack, or judge. You find a natural patience and acceptance not only for the other person but also for the things you are thinking and feeling.

This is how true compassion and love begin to infuse every relationship. The key is to start practicing now with everyone with whom you come in contact.

Resistance and Conflict

As you go about using this practice, you may still find yourself triggered by some people. You may experience resistance or conflict. It's okay. Use the experience as a way to go deeper into natural rest. Everyone who triggers you becomes your teacher.

Resistance is energy that arises in the present moment in the form of thought, emotion, or some sensation within the body.

It may be a thought that says something or someone should be different, or that someone should stop doing what they're doing or saying what they're saying.

Resistance sometimes arises as the energy of emotion in the body, without any thought accompanying it.

When resistance arises in any form in a relationship, simply notice it and take a moment to rest in presence.

If resistance arises in thought, notice those words or pictures and bring attention into the space of the inner body. Let any emotions be as they are in that space without mentally labeling them. Let them be until they dissolve away. And if they do not dissolve away, stay aware of them, allowing them to be as they are.

If resistance arises only as energy in the body (such as an emotion or sensation), without thought, recognize the peripheral space around the energy as you feel into it. Let the energy be in that space completely without trying to fix it or make it go away. This is acceptance.

Sometimes interaction results in conflict. The practice is the same—notice, feel, rest. Some people falsely believe that resting with whatever arises will render them unable to respond effectively to other people. This really isn't the case. In fact, being more aware of your own thoughts and feelings and allowing them to be can often help you respond more effectively. This practice brings more space to your experience and more space in your relationships. These practices are not about becoming a welcome mat for people to walk all over. You will find yourself able to respond appropriately. Many report being able to respond and express themselves much more clearly and easily after doing this work for several years.

The Need to Be Right

The need to be right in relationships is often a source of conflict.

The need to be right arises from emphasizing thoughts for a sense of self rather than relaxing into restful presence.

The need to be right appears when there's a difference in viewpoints. Regardless of the content of the different viewpoints, the subtext is always the same: "I'm right and you're wrong!" This is an automatic, unconscious response when we take ourselves to be a thought-based self-center.

Being right strengthens the self-center, placing stress on our relationships. When we emphasize the need to be right, we live in isolation and separation from one another.

In these moments, there's an unconscious assumption happening. The assumption is that our identity is contained within thought. By being right, our sense of self is protected, preserved, and strengthened. Being wrong threatens this self-image.

Nothing needs to be analyzed about the need to be right.

Our real identities don't reside in temporary thoughts. So there's nothing to defend with regard to thought. There's nothing to fight about.

Through resting in presence, we find the need to be right diminishes automatically.

No complicated analysis is needed—only simple rest and watching feelings and thoughts come and go! Don't worry, you will still be able to respond and express your viewpoint—but with less attachment to it.

Any emotional energy or sense of diminishment from being made wrong is allowed to simply be in the space of the inner body. This energy transforms itself into presence.

Presence transforms relationships. It allows all mental and emotional energy to be as it is. It allows others with whom we make contact to relax their need to be right.

Relationships become infused with rest. A natural ease of being permeates each encounter with each person.

We may still take action to help others, or change or leave unhealthy situations. We may still explain to others that their behavior is unacceptable. But our response is coming from the natural, selfless wisdom of presence, not from self-centeredness.

Taking the Perspectives of Others

We may find a deep peace through presence. We may see through a lot of our own concepts and stories. We may no longer find the need to incessantly emphasize these concepts and stories.

In this seeing, we want to be mindful of the temptation to tune other people out. Presence isn't about ignoring others' stories. When we tune other people out as they're speaking, we're using thought-free presence as a way to cut ourselves off from life and from others. This is just more escape.

Presence carries a natural capacity to listen without judgment and condemnation of what others are saying.

Presence is already awake and alert, listening to what's appearing.

All we have to do is notice this alertness.

All sounds, words, ideas, and stories appear and disappear within a deep silence.

In all conversations, we listen from silence. Silence is openness.

Simply resting as silent presence allows us to listen fully to what others are saying. This reveals a natural compassion within us.

Within presence, we find a natural capacity to take another's perspective completely and nonjudgmentally.

As someone begins speaking, we allow her words to create concepts within the mind. We notice the thought-free presence of our basic identity is like a blank screen on which her words paint a picture.

As we're listening, we become her story. We put ourselves in her position, as the main character in her story. This is "perspective taking." We're taking the perspective of the speaker.

We don't listen to her story to simply agree or disagree or to give advice, although that can happen.

To be open when someone is speaking doesn't mean that we never disagree with what she's saying. Disagreement happens. But in noticing that we're disagreeing, we become aware of the viewpoint we're emphasizing.

By letting that viewpoint come and go, without emphasizing it, we can relax again into nonjudgmental, quiet, listening presence.

This clear, quiet mind is the true listener within us. From this place, we're able to take the perspective of the person speaking.

In listening from nonjudgmental presence, we're able to notice whenever we're agreeing with others just to please them. People pleasing is self-centered. We're more interested in people liking us than in really hearing what they're saying.

In perspective taking, we listen for listening's sake. We listen for the sake of inhabiting the speaker's story from her point of view. We listen from nonjudgmental silence. Our main interest isn't agreement, disagreement, or even neutrality. Our interest is taking the perspective of the one who's speaking. For that moment, we become the speaker.

In perspective taking, we allow the speaker's words to become a movie within our minds, regardless of whether the story is pleasant or unpleasant, or whether it feels right or wrong. We allow each scene to play out completely. She's the director and producer. We're merely the screen for her script.

If she begins telling us about her day, we allow those words to create the story of her day as it's playing out. We feel into her emotions as best we can.

If she's explaining the frustration she experienced while arguing with her husband, we place ourselves there, in her shoes, during the argument. We look from her eyes as she tells the story. We see her husband from her point of view. In that moment, we see everything from her point of view.

If she's telling the story of how wonderful it was to walk in the park on a cool autumn morning, we place ourselves there, in her shoes, walking through the park, seeing the beauty of nature through her eyes.

Every person we meet becomes a new perspective for us to take. We come to see that life contains many perspectives.

Perspective taking is a deeply compassionate form of sharing. It's true sympathetic listening, unencumbered by judgment and criticism. It opens us up to seeing life from many angles. It opens us up to the unconditional love already present within us.

The possibilities are limitless in perspective taking. A partner can take the perspective of his significant other. A defendant in a criminal case can take the perspective of the judge. A mother can take the perspective of her addicted son. A Christian can take the perspective of a Muslim.

A twenty-year-old can take the perspective of a sixty-year-old. Someone completely healthy can take the perspective of someone dying of cancer. A male can take the perspective of a female. Someone who's heterosexual can take the perspective of someone who's gay or lesbian. A heroin addict can take the perspective of a shopping addict.

When we open up in this way, we stop looking at life from within a self-centered lens. We start looking from what we really are—selfless love. We see that presence takes a vast array of forms and that only our stories separate us. In selfless love, the boundaries between us are seen to be conceptual only and so they dissolve.

When we don't take the perspectives of others, and we only look from our own perspective, we live in a self-centered reality. We consult only our own thoughts. We dismiss those who disagree with us or present a different interpretation. When we meet people, we're meeting interpretations of life that are very different from ours. In self-centeredness, each person lives in his or her own reality.

It's only the emphasis on thought that separates us, making us feel as though we live in separate realities.

As we're taking the perspective of another, we may find that a certain response is necessary or that there's something we feel we need to say in order to help the person speaking.

We may still find it necessary to agree or disagree or give advice. This is perfectly fine. We retain the ability to use our discriminating minds when necessary.

When we do respond, we respond from presence. By resting in presence before, during, and after our response, the response comes from selflessness. It's naturally infused with rest, wisdom, love, and compassion. It isn't coming from the seeking, controlling, and manipulating energy of the self-center. It isn't coming from a need to be right. It's coming from openness.

We know that when we're speaking, we aren't being objective. We're merely stating a single, limited, subjective point of view, conditioned by our particular language, personal history, values, and cultural, religious, and philosophical framework.

In selfless presence, we're fine whether or not other people listen to us or take our suggestions and advice. We lose the need to be heard and be right. We find a natural desire to hear and remain open. These attributes don't need to be cultivated through effort. They arise naturally through making restful presence the most important thing in our lives.

In the openness of presence, there's nothing we need to change about others or ourselves. We simply rest in selfless presence, listening without judgment and responding naturally from that presence.

Key Points

The following key points will help you review the role of relationship in addiction and recovery:

We are in relationship with everyone and everything. Our relationships to people, objects, and events mirror back who we are. Understanding this is key before reading and practicing the tools in chapter 6.

Bring natural rest into all human relationships. Use the practices in this book when interacting with other humans. Be the open, present space that allows others to be who they are. Notice your own thoughts and feel emotions directly as they arise. This will help you to respond with love and compassion rather than with fear, defense, or attack. It helps to dissolve resistance and conflict as well as the need to be right.

Take the perspective of others. Whenever someone is speaking to you, and while you are resting in presence, allow the other person's perspective to paint words, pictures, and energies in your own awareness, as if you are experiencing what he is experiencing. This helps bring compassion to your responses to him.

CHAPTER 6

The Living Inquiries

As stated in the introduction, the Living Inquiries are the *most potent* tools in this book. Many people have discovered freedom using these tools. They free us from our addiction to self and from the disharmony and imbalance we experience in certain relationships with other people. If used correctly, they work very well to clear away the stories that lead us into addiction and keep us addicted.

In the previous chapter, I discussed how relationship plays a vital role in your identity, behavior, thoughts, and feelings. The Inquiries will help you gain insight and freedom in all of your relationships—not just your relationships with other people, but also your relationship to thoughts, feelings, sensations, and addictive substances and activities. Everything you have learned and practiced so far in this book has laid the foundation for you to go deeper into this work through these Inquiries. The tools of natural rest, noticing thoughts, and directly experiencing bodily energies are all built into the Inquiries. Take your time with this chapter. Learn the mechanics of each inquiry. Try each one out on your own. Practice!

If you have difficulty using the Inquiries on your own, I highly recommend working with one of my trained Living Inquiries facilitators. They are trained to help you see things about yourself that you may not be able to see on your own, and to guide you through the untangling of negative beliefs and addictive behaviors.

For more information about the Inquiries and to find a facilitator, visit http://www.livinginquiries.com.

The Compulsion Inquiry

An effective tool for reducing or eliminating the cravings for, or compulsive use of, substances and activities is the Compulsion Inquiry (the "CI").

The CI targets compulsion directly. Before you reach for an addictive substance or activity, an unconscious, ghostlike mental picture (the "ghost image") flashes quickly in and out of awareness. That picture appears as a future thought associated with indulging in the addictive substance or activity. The picture creates a strong, almost instantaneous, body-mind compulsion to use the substance or activity.

The CI helps to undo the Velcro Effect between the thoughts and energies behind an addiction.

How the Compulsion Inquiry Works

The Compulsion Inquiry, like each of the Inquiries in this chapter, is all about slowing down your interior experience of words, pictures, and bodily energy and isolating each element. Once the element is isolated, you rest and observe it for a bit, then you ask this question: "Is this set of words, this picture, or this energy the command to engage in the substance or activity?"

If you are looking at a mental image of a mug of beer, you ask, "Is this image the command to drink beer?" Don't answer with your intellect. Answer from your body. Don't rush through the process, either. Rest with and allow whatever you are experiencing. If you feel any emotion or sensation velcroed to the picture, then the answer is yes. You then bring attention to that bodily energy, after the mental image dissolves away. You then ask, "Is this sensation, by itself, the command to drink beer?" You continue through each element—each set of words, each mental picture, and each bodily energy—looking for the command. When you isolate these elements in this way, you often cannot find a command in any of the isolated elements. The compulsion to use then falls away.

An Example of the Compulsion Inquiry

This example comes from an actual experience I had when the CI was first developed. In this example, I am facilitating myself through the CI:

One day, while walking in the hot sun, I noticed a coffee shop and I knew that they sold bottled water there. I was thirsty! As I walked in the door of the shop, I immediately noticed a glimmering glass counter within which sat several rows of colorful, beautifully decorated donuts and other baked goods. I felt a pull toward the glass counter. As I stood before the glass, I felt my mouth watering and imagined eating a red velvet cupcake—one of my vices at the time.

Instead of blindly ordering a cupcake, I sat down at a table in the back of the shop and began using the CI. I noticed a ghost image of the cupcake in my mind. I slowed that image down and isolated it. Resting in presence, I kept my attention on the image for quite a while, allowing it to float freely in the peripheral space around it.

Eventually, I asked, "Is there a command on this picture to eat that cupcake?" The answer was a clear yes because I felt a sensation velcroed to the image. I didn't ask my mind. I let my body answer. I then allowed the image to be in awareness until it began to dissolve away.

Bringing attention into my body, I rested with the sensation, noticing the peripheral space around it. I sat there for a bit before asking another question. Eventually, I asked, "Is this sensation, by itself, the command to eat a cupcake?" At first, the answer seemed to be no because I noticed no words or pictures with it. That's how we answer the question with regard to an emotion or sensation. If there are no words or pictures connected to it, it's a no. If there are any words or pictures connected to it, it's a yes.

Even though a no came up, as I sat with the sensation longer, I began to notice some words arising. The words were *What's the harm in just eating one cupcake?* I spelled those words out in my mind, actually seeing all the letters of the words. I allowed that set of words to float freely, keeping my attention on them. I wasn't looking at the meaning of the words, only the appearance of them (how they looked). I then asked, "Is there a command on those words to eat a cupcake?" The answer was yes because I felt that sensation in the body connected to the words.

After allowing the words to be witnessed until they dissolved away on their own, I returned attention to the sensation in the body. But, at this point, both the cupcake picture and the words had fallen away. All that was left was this sensation. I rested with it. Allowed it. I even said, "Thank you for arising. I love you. Stay as long as you like." This helped relax some of the resistance to the sensation.

As I sat with the sensation, feeling into it, I asked, "Is this sensation, by itself, the command to eat a cupcake?" This time there were no more words or pictures connected to it. It was just a sensation all by itself. The answer was no. I allowed the sensation to be there for quite a while. I refused to go back to the counter until the sensation had dissolved completely.

As I returned to the counter, I noticed that I had lost interest in the cupcake. The command couldn't be found in my inquiry. It's as if the pull toward the cupcake had vanished. I ordered a bottle of water, walked out the door, and enjoyed the rest of my day, knowing that I had used this work in an effective way. I felt much better without the cupcake.

Notes About the Compulsion Inquiry

The Compulsion Inquiry can be done with any substance or activity. You can look for the command in anything that involves *a compulsive movement toward the future*, including toward alcohol, a drug, pornography, obsessive cleaning of your house, or anything else.

If the word "command" does not resonate with you, you can substitute it with some other word that does resonate— like urge, drive, impulse, need, or desire. You just have to find a word that really captures what compulsion really feels like in your own experience.

If you find yourself overcomplicating the Compulsion Inquiry, just remember this: *three elements, one question*. There are only three elements to look at (words, pictures, and bodily energy). Remember, energy is either emotion or sensation. There is only one question to ask ("Is there a command on this element to drink, eat, smoke, shoot up—whatever?").

If that version of the question does not resonate with you, you can change the form of the question to any of the following: "Where is the command on those words (to drink beer)?" "Where is the command in that picture (to drink beer)?" "Where is the command in that energy (to drink beer)?"

If you have difficulty with the CI on your own, work with a facilitator first. Sessions with a facilitator can help tremendously, allowing you to eventually go solo with the CI.

The Unfindable Inquiry

The Unfindable Inquiry (UI) is a unique tool that can be used to see through the sense of separation in whatever form it takes. At first, it may be a bit daunting to attempt this inquiry on your own. If you have difficulty, find someone in your Natural Rest group or a facilitator who has experience with this particular inquiry to guide you. Once you get a feel for how it works, you can then begin using it on your own. When used properly, the UI is very effective.

The UI can be used in many different ways, as you'll see below. It can be used to see through the sense of a separate self—which means to see the "emptiness" of the self. It can also be used to see the emptiness of another person with whom you're in a relationship, or a substance or activity toward which you feel a craving or addiction. The word "emptiness" refers to the fact that, when you actually look for a separate, permanent person or thing, you find only words, pictures, and energies appearing, one after another. The object is actually *unfindable* as something separate from these temporary arisings.

The seemingly physical nature of bodies and other objects can be tricky. It can seem, when you first start doing inquiry, that physical bodies and things are more than words, pictures, and energy. For example, touching a chest makes it appear that you are touching a solid, separate person. Seeing colors and shapes everywhere seems to prove that reality is made of separate things. But having a facilitator guide you through the process helps a lot. Facilitators can show you in your own direct experience that touch and vision are sensations only and that words and mental pictures play a key role in the belief that people and things are separate.

Don't try to understand what is being said here intellectually. The UI is an experiential approach. Reach out to a facilitator. You'll be glad you did. Or try it on your own. Either way, just try it. Practice it, often. This experiential approach is quite freeing because addiction and suffering come directly from the belief in separation, and the UI is designed to help you see through that belief.

Many people begin using the UI on certain deficiency stories, which are identities that we carry around—such as *I'm not good enough, I'm a failure, I'm unlovable,* or *I'm unsafe.* I suggest starting with deficiency stories. These stories tend to fuel addiction as we attempt to cover up, medicate, or escape the pain of these stories. When we believe a deficiency story, we believe this is what we are, fundamentally. Deficiency stories become our identity, as if there is a self at the core of our being that is fundamentally deficient. Uprooting and dissolving these false stories can be very freeing. See the subsection below, titled "The Boomerang," to better understand how to work with deficiency stories.

How the Unfindable Inquiry Works

Here are the steps:

1. Name the object that appears to be separate.

2. Try to find the object. Go through each of the main words, pictures, and bodily energies (one by one) that make up the object. For each appearance ask, "Is this it?" (Are these words the object? Is this emotion the object? Is this sensation the object?) If you're looking for the separate self, you may substitute the words "Is this it?" with "Is this me?"

Just remember: *Name it, then find it.*

An Example of the Unfindable Inquiry

In this example of the UI, Matt is being guided by a facilitator.

Facilitator: Name the object you would like to try and find.

Matt: I'd like to find me. I'm the root of my problems.

Facilitator: Okay, but let's be a little more specific. There are millions of selves in the world; who do you take yourself to be, exactly?

Matt: I've always thought of myself as a failure. I'm never going to succeed. I'm miserable most of the time. Yesterday is a good example. I sat around all day just feeling sorry for myself.

Facilitator: So let's say that the object you're trying to find is "Matt," the person who is a failure. Try to find it. Rest in presence and listen to the voice in your head as it says the word *Matt*. Is the word "Matt," you—the failure?"

Matt: No, that's just a name, just a word.

Facilitator: How about the words *I'm never going to succeed?* Is that you—the failure?

Matt: Is that me? No, that's just a thought, too.

Facilitator: Be careful not to answer only with the intellect. Look directly with awareness. And remember to pay attention to your body. Does the body react in some way when you see or hear the words *I'm never going to succeed?* If the body reacts in any way, say yes. If it doesn't, say no.

Matt: Yes, there is sadness and a contraction in my chest.

Facilitator: Observe the words *I'm never going to succeed* until they fade away. As they fade away, rest in thought-free presence. Bring attention to the raw energy of sadness and contraction, without labeling it. Take your time.

Matt: Okay, I'm sitting with that energy.

Facilitator: Is that energy, by itself, you—the failure?

Matt: No, that energy is not the failure. And it just dissipated once I saw that.

Facilitator: Did you see how the words *I'm never going to succeed* initially felt stuck to the emotion?

Matt: Yes.

Facilitator: That's the Velcro Effect. You allowed the emotion to be as it is, without the words, and that released the Velcro Effect. Did you notice that?

Matt: Yes. Very nice. Most of my life I've just stayed in the story instead of feeling the emotions directly.

Facilitator: Now I want you to take a moment and rest in presence again. This time, look directly at the words *I'm a failure.* Do you see those words?

Matt: Yes.

Facilitator: Are the words *I'm a failure* you?

Matt: Yes, those words are me. They feel really close... too close. The sadness is back.

Facilitator: Let those words fall away on their own, and feel the raw energy of the emotion without a label for it. Is that energy, by itself, the failure?

Matt: Yes. For some reason, those words really feel stuck to the emotion.

Facilitator: That's okay. Take this pen and paper and write down the words *I'm a failure*. Then look at the words on the paper. Are those words *you?*

Matt: Now I can see that they're just words. No, those words are not the actual failure. The emotion released as soon as I saw that.

Facilitator: Put the words *I'm miserable most of the time* in a picture frame in your mind. Are those words you—the self that's a failure?

Matt: Yes, that definitely feels like me. The sadness and contraction are back.

Facilitator: Look at the words "sadness" and "contraction." Are those words, by themselves, the failure?

Matt: No, those words are not it, not me. But the words *I'm miserable most of the time* seem like they are me, the failure.

Facilitator: Whenever any thought *feels* like the object you're trying to find in this inquiry, it always means that some emotion or sensation is arising along with the thought. Emotions and sensations are like alarm bells reminding you to be in your body, and to feel the emotions directly. So let all words and pictures come to rest by observing them. Bring attention directly to the nameless energy in your chest. Take as much time as you need. Relax and let that energy be as it is. Notice the peripheral space around the energy. Is that energy you, the failure?

Matt: That energy feels like me.

Facilitator: Okay, whenever an emotion or sensation feels like the self, it just means that some thought (some words or a mental picture) is arising along with it. That's the Velcro Effect. What words or pictures appear?

Matt: It's a memory of me losing my last job.

Facilitator: Okay, that's a picture. Look directly at the picture of you losing your job. Is that picture, by itself, you, the failure?

Matt: No, that's not the failure. The picture just faded.

Facilitator: You mentioned that you sat around yesterday feeling sorry for yourself. Look at those words. Are those words, by themselves, the failure?

Matt: No.

Facilitator: Look at the picture (the memory) of you sitting around yesterday feeling sorry for yourself. Is that picture you?

Matt: I can see that it's a picture, but it feels like a failure. The sadness and contraction came up again.

Facilitator: Are the words "sadness" and "contraction" you, the failure?

Matt: No, those are just words.

Facilitator: Be aware of the sadness and contraction but without naming or labeling them. Is that energy you?

Matt: No, that's not me. But that energy feels stuck.

Facilitator: Whenever energy feels stuck in the body, that means there's still identification happening with our thoughts. Sometimes the thoughts appear as mental pictures instead of words. These mental pictures are being projected by the mind onto the sensation or emotion. Close your eyes and tell me if you see any mental pictures.

Matt: Yes, it feels like the energy is contained in a knot. I see a picture of the knot.

Facilitator: Look just at the picture of the knot by itself. Place no words on it. Gently observe the picture without describing it. Imagine it in a picture frame, if that helps. Is that picture you, the failure?

Matt: No, I can see it's just a picture and it just vanished. Now the sadness is welling up.

Facilitator: As all words and pictures vanish, just experience that energy, letting it be exactly as it is. Take your time... Is that energy you?

Matt: Wow, no! It just moved through. I can see now that when no words or pictures are placed on emotion. It's not a failure. I don't feel like a failure.

Facilitator: Just rest in presence now, letting anything and everything arise and fall naturally. Can you find the self who's a failure?

Matt: I cannot find the failure. I see some faint words and pictures coming through, but they feel light and empty. In fact, I cannot find a self. This is so simple and effective. And so freeing... I've literally been thinking of myself as something I cannot find when I really look.

Facilitator: Great! Whenever you find yourself telling the story that you're a failure, first try and rest in presence without emphasizing those thoughts. Feel the energy in the body without labeling it. If you still find yourself telling the story, try to find the failure using this inquiry.

Matt: I will. This is a great tool!

A FEW HELPFUL TIPS

Let's go back over the inquiry above and add some tips that may help as you begin doing this inquiry on your own. For the tips below, put yourself in place of Matt. When you do the inquiry on your own story, you might not choose "failure" as the thing you take yourself to be. Choose something that feels true for you.

Simplify thoughts down to either words or pictures. If you look into your experience, you can see that thoughts arise in one of two different ways—words or pictures. Words are literally things like *Matt* or *I am a failure*. Pictures are mental images that arise to awareness, such as the picture (in other words, memory) of sitting and feeling sorry for yourself, or the picture of a body part or a knot. It's good to see the difference between words and pictures and to notice exactly which of these are arising to give you the sense of a separate self.

It may also be helpful to frame the particular words or pictures. For example, imagine the words *I'm miserable most of the time* inside a picture frame in your mind. Stare right at the content in the frame and then ask, "Is this me—the failure?" It may also be helpful to write the words down.

Refrain from trying to answer the question "Is this it?" intellectually. Notice that the facilitator requested that Matt not answer intellectually. Don't think about your answer. Don't analyze the question. Don't refer to other parts of your story to find the answer. Just look, presently, at one thought only. Look at the thought in the way you would look at a color without naming the color. Look directly, with thought-free observation. From that direct observation, ask, "Is this me—the failure?" Intellectually, you may see that this is just a thought, and not the object (failure). *But always pay attention to your body during the inquiry.* Notice when the body reacts with an emotion or sensation. This is the body's way of letting you know that, on some level, you believe that you're that thought. If the body reacts, answer yes. If it doesn't react, answer no.

Keep your answer to the question "Is this me?" to a simple yes or no. Don't add detailed analysis to the answer. For example, if you're truly a failure, and that failure is here, present in and as your body and mind, it shouldn't be hard to find. You should be able to find it right away, in your direct, present experience, without the need to elaborate. Take the example of looking for a pair of shoes in a closet. If you pick up a shirt, there's no need to give five reasons why the shirt isn't a pair of shoes. You know that it's not. No elaboration is needed; you just keep looking for the shoes. Treat this inquiry the same way. Stick to trying to find the object, with a simple yes or no.

Remember that you're looking for the object—not evidence of it, thoughts that point to it, or parts of it. During the inquiry, it may seem as if every temporary thought, emotion, and sensation you encounter is "part of" the object, evidence of it, or pointing to it. Don't settle for this kind of thinking! Go deeper. *Look for the object itself.* If all these temporary things point to it, where are *you*—the real, permanent, separate, actual failure? If all words describe it, where are *you*? If these appearances are merely part of it, where are *you*? The *you*—the actual failure—is what you're looking for. And that's precisely what cannot be found when you do this inquiry.

For example, if you're looking for the failure you take yourself to be, it may seem as if the thought *I'm never going to succeed* is part of the failure. Forget about finding parts. Look for the failure itself. Is the thought *I'm never going to succeed* you—the actual failure? That's the proper question. We often assume that these kinds of thoughts are describing or pointing to an actual, inherent failure that's *really there* under the thoughts. To prove that the failure isn't there under the thoughts, drop any thought that seems to describe or point to the failure. Notice that whenever you drop these thoughts, you can't find the failure. And, of course, you can't find it when the thoughts are there, either. You find only thoughts about a failure, one after the other—but no actual failure.

If you're looking at a thought and the thought seems to be the object, it always means that there's some sensation or emotion arising with the thought. If the body reacts in any way to the question "Is this thought me?" just say, "Yes, this is me." Then bring your thought-free attention immediately into the body and experience the emotion or sensation directly, letting it be exactly as it is, without trying to change or get rid of it. If you find your mind labeling the emotion or sensation with words such as "sadness" or "contraction," ask yourself, "Is the word *sadness* me?" "Is the word "contraction" me?" Then relax all thoughts for a few seconds, and experience the energy of the emotion or sensation, without any labels.

Simply sit with the raw sensory experience itself, resting in thought-free presence. And then ask, "Is this energy, by itself, me—the failure?" If you see that it's not the failure, let it be as it is, without trying to change or get rid of it. This frees up the energy to move and change naturally, often dissolving on its own. But the point isn't to try and get rid of or resist anything. That's just more seeking. The point is to see that the energy is *not* the failure. Once you see that no thought, emotion, or sensation is the object, it no longer matters whether these things arise. Any appearance can come and go, yet the failure is never found. This allows the story and emotions to quiet naturally and effortlessly. Suffering, seeking, and conflict show up in our experience as a result of unconsciously believing that these appearances form a separate object.

If an emotion or sensation in the body seems to be the object, it always means that there is a thought arising along with the sensation or emotion. If this happens, observe the thought stream to see which thought (which words or picture) is coming up with the sensation or emotion. Then look directly at that thought and ask, "Is this me?" An emotion or sensation only *seems* like the object when any identifying thought like *This is me* arises along with it.

Pay particular attention to the subtle mental pictures, such as images of body parts and other forms and shapes, which appear to contain certain emotions and sensations. If you see any picture whenever you're experiencing emotions and sensations, ask whether that picture *is* the object. For example, is this picture of a knot *the failure?* As you begin to see that these are just mental images, and not the object, the pictures tend to change or disappear on their own. Even if they stick around, it won't matter much, once you see that they're, indeed, not the failure.

Once the words and pictures have dissolved around any emotion or sensation, remember to ask "Is this emotion, by itself, me—the failure?" or "Is this sensation, by itself, me—the failure?" and then let the emotion or sensation be as it is, without words or pictures. At that point, the energy will either stay, change, or dissolve. Either way, this allows you to see that the energy is *just energy*. It's not a failure. Be careful to remember this step. In not remembering this step, you ignore bodily energy and keep the inquiries on a superficial or mental level only. Addiction is all about escaping or medicating bodily energies. Sitting with bodily energies, by themselves, and letting them be as they are is very helpful when it comes to releasing addiction. By including this step every time, we are essentially retraining our system to no longer escape or medicate these bodily energies.

When you are working with a facilitator, you may find that the facilitator refers to all emotions and sensations as "energies," or some other all-inclusive label. In this case, "energies" refers to *anything* felt in the body—including emotions such as anger, sadness, or fear, as well as sensations such as tightness, pain, pleasure, or contraction. The facilitator is making no distinction between emotions and sensations. Putting all bodily energy into one category can help to simplify the process of looking. After all, when there are no labels on bodily energies, it's all just energy. Once simplified in this way, you can see that your entire experience is broken down into three categories (words, pictures, and energies) rather than the four categories previously discussed (words, pictures, sensations, and emotions). You may also simplify your experience down to these three categories when doing the Living Inquiries on your own, or you may break it down to words, pictures, sensations, and emotions. Use whatever works best for you.

Undo the Velcro Effect

Whenever you think you're experiencing a separate object, notice that the thoughts, emotions, and sensations seem stuck together. That's the Velcro Effect. For example, when the thought *I'm a failure* arises, it can feel as if sadness is stuck to the thought.

Really picking apart each thought, emotion, and sensation and then asking "Is this me?" for each one is a powerful way of untangling the sense that thoughts, emotions, and sensations are stuck together. In seeing that no thought, emotion, or sensation is, by itself, the object, the Velcro Effect comes undone. The emptiness of the failure identity (or whatever object you're inquiring into) is now seen.

Once you do this inquiry a few times, you may no longer need to ask the question, "Is this me?" You may begin to see that this inquiry is just another way of pointing you to the direct experience of resting in presence and seeing that all energies arise and fall, never forming a separate object (a separate self).

Keep It Simple: Three Elements, One Question

As with the Compulsion Inquiry, you can keep the Unfindable Inquiry simple by remembering this: *three elements, one question.* For all the inquiries, there are only three elements to look at (words, pictures, and energy). Energy includes both emotion and sensation. There is only one question stated in different ways:

"Are those words me, the victim?"

"Is that picture me, the victim?"

"Is this energy me, the victim?"

Keeping it that simple keeps the mind out of the game. This is a direct looking for a self or other thing.

Using the Unfindable Inquiry on Addictive Substances and Activities

You can use the Unfindable Inquiry on anything to which you feel addicted (for example, a drug, a glass of wine, a casino, or the Internet). Addiction is all about separation. Separation creates the sense that there's a separate person, here, who must indulge in a separate object, out there, in order to feel complete or whole. Using the UI on substances and activities helps the mind withdraw from fixation on the addictive substance or activity itself.

Let's say your substance of choice is a martini. Each day, around 5:00 p.m., you begin craving a martini. You find your body unconsciously moving to the kitchen and your hands pulling out the glass and making the martini. You drink one after another, until you fall asleep or pass out. This is like being asleep to your desire for the drink, as if on autopilot.

Now let's take a look at that entire sequence from another angle. Using the UI, you begin to wake up in the midst of the desire itself by trying to find the object (martini) in words, pictures, and bodily energies.

The moment you have the thought *I want a martini*, rest in presence and look directly at the words. Ask: "Are those words, by themselves, the martini?" If your response is no, you can just keep looking for the martini in whatever words, pictures, and energies that arise. But if your response is yes, notice that energy (some emotion or sensation) is arising in the body along with those words.

Now bring thought-free attention to the sensation or emotion. Maybe it's a craving, or anxiety. Rest and experience the sensation without the words "I want a martini," and without all other words and pictures. Is that sensation itself the martini when you aren't labeling it? Notice it as nameless energy. This energy, when you aren't adding words and pictures to it, comes and goes. It relaxes. Yet, even if it doesn't relax, you can see that the energy isn't the martini. Remember: If any emotion or sensation feels like the object, it means there's a thought arising. Look at the thought and see that it's not the martini.

Taking brief moments of thought-free presence, in between the questions, helps a lot during this inquiry. Notice that, during the few seconds of relaxing without thoughts, nothing is needed. In that moment, life is complete just as it is. Sensations and emotions may be coming through, but for a few seconds, at least, they aren't hooking into any stories about desiring a martini.

As you're resting, look again for the martini in the next words, pictures, or energies that arise. Don't actively make thoughts appear. Just relax and notice when they arise naturally, and then look again. Maybe this time you see a mental picture of the bottle sitting inside the cabinet. Look directly at that mental picture. Ask yourself, "Is that picture *it?*" Notice that it's just a picture. Let the picture change or relax on its own, once you see it for what it is.

Notice that you cannot find the martini in any individual words, pictures, or energies, no matter how thoroughly you look. Even if you end up grabbing a martini, look to see if the color or texture of the bottle, or any other sensation of taste or smell, by itself, is the martini. None of those energies, by themselves, are the martini.

A martini never "calls your name." It doesn't contain any magnetic pull on its own. One person can become addicted to martinis while another person can feel repulsed by them. The magnetic pull is an illusion created by misperceiving your experience. A martini doesn't exist solely on its own accord. The martini craving arises by way of thoughts, emotions, and sensations that seem welded together. The mind creates an association between well-being and what it perceives as the source of that well-being—a martini. This misperception results in the brain's pleasure center being hijacked, creating a repetitive urge to drink, over and over each night. Interrupt that association by using this inquiry each time you feel the urge to drink.

During the inquiry, as you move back and forth between words, pictures, or energies (one by one), these appearances feel less and less welded together. The words and mental pictures of the martini start to feel weaker. They begin to dissolve more quickly each time you look at them. The emotions and sensations that arise with these thoughts are more easily experienced without labels.

This makes the object of your desire appear emptier and more transparent in your perception. You're able to witness the words and pictures more, instead of unconsciously following the trail of these thoughts like a straight line to the vodka bottle. You discover that what you were seeing in your mind as a martini calling your name is more like a movie. Yet now the movie is conscious. You're no longer asleep in the desire. It's now easier to rest in presence. In that restfulness, you're seeing through the sense of separation that lies at the heart of addiction.

Instead of doing the UI on the martini, you can do it on "the person who desires a martini." Try to find yourself. Is the thought *I want a martini* you? No, it's just a thought. How about the mental image of you drinking a martini later in the day—is that you, the person who desires a martini? No, it's just a picture. How about the craving in your chest or stomach when you don't label it? Is that you—the person who wants a martini? No, it's just nameless energy.

The Boomerang

It's not always easy to name the deficiency story that lies at the root of our addictions or suffering. The Boomerang can help.

As stated above, most people carry a deficiency story that strikes at the very heart of who they think they are. It's the core story of the self-center. This core story is some version of "there is something wrong with me." It comes in many forms: "I'm unlovable," "I'm not good enough," "I'm lacking," "I'm incomplete," "I'm not 'there' yet," "I'm wrong," "I'm weak," "I'm unsafe," "I'm insecure," "I'm imperfect," or "I'm inadequate." And that's just the short list. The form it takes is unique to each individual.

The core deficient self is a false script about ourselves that we carry around in life, from childhood into adulthood. It's an offshoot of a belief in being separate. There really isn't a core deficient, separate self. We just believe there is. We're carrying around a fundamental lie about who we really are. There's a palpable emotional aspect to this lie, a wound that gets triggered when other people seem to mirror this story back to us. This lie hurts. It's responsible for much of the difficulty we experience in relationships.

RELATIONSHIP AS MIRROR

As stated in the last chapter, relationship has a built-in mirroring effect. As we move through life, other people appear to reflect back to us this core, deficient self. When this sense of deficiency is triggered in relationship, an emotional wound arises. If the pain seems like too much, we may find ourselves trying to avoid it, to blame others for it, or to medicate it somehow by reaching for addictive substances or activities. There's a tendency to focus our attention outward toward others, as if they're the source of the pain. But others are just a mirror showing us what we believe about ourselves. Here are a few signs indicating that we're carrying a belief in self-deficiency:

Insisting on being right and making others wrong

Seeking love, praise, attention, acknowledgment, or approval

Comparing ourselves to others as better or worse

Belittling, ridiculing, or bullying others

Trying to control or manipulate others

Judging others negatively or complaining about them

Alienating ourselves and avoiding certain painful relationships

Acting on selfish ambition

Feeling jealous or envious of others

Much of this mind activity is based in fear of looking directly at who we've falsely taken *ourselves* to be—deficient in some way. The others in our lives are constantly mirroring this illusion of self back to us.

If you look, the mirroring effect is happening in every direction. The view of others as successful often mirrors back an "unsuccessful self." When a loved one doesn't respond to you the way you expected, or a romantic relationship ends, this often mirrors back an "unlovable self." Attractive people may mirror back an "unattractive self." People who look important in the world may mirror back an "unimportant self" or "unworthy self." When someone judges or criticizes you, this may mirror back a self that feels wrong. When others appear arrogant or authoritative, this may reflect back a weak, insignificant, or small self. If others appear powerful, you may feel less powerful or powerless.

It's not just other people. Anything can reflect deficiency back to you. An addiction to a drug or some other thing mirrors back a self that's lacking or "not enough." Future things such as enlightenment, recovery, and self-improvement may point back to a self that seems presently incomplete.

The Boomerang adds an additional step to the Unfindable Inquiry, and we use it on the core deficiency story as it shows up in relationship.

Like a boomerang that returns back to the thrower, the deficient self is reflected back to you in relationship. The Boomerang focuses on seeing that mirroring effect and then, with the UI, seeing through the deficient self that's being mirrored or reflected back. The relationship could be with anything—any person, place, event, goal, or other thing. When we really believe that we're deficient at the core, almost everything in our lives can appear to confirm this story.

How the Boomerang Works

The following steps outline how to use the Boomerang in conjunction with the Unfindable Inquiry:

1. *Use the mirror.* Whenever you're triggered in relationship, find out what deficiency story this person or thing is mirroring back to you. (There's an example of how to do this below.)

2. *Name it.* Give the deficient self a specific name (such as "unlovable self," "unfulfilled self," "lacking self," "incomplete self," "broken self," "unsuccessful self," "unsafe self," "invalid self," and so on). Whatever you pick, make sure it feels true for you, as if that is what you really are at the core.

3. *Find it.* Once you name that deficient self, try to find it using the UI.

You can see that the Boomerang is very similar to the Unfindable Inquiry. Steps 2 and 3 are the same "name it" and "find it" elements from the UI. The Boomerang simply adds a new first step—using the mirror of relationship to identify the core deficiency story that is being triggered within you in a particular relationship scenario. The Boomerang applies whenever you're looking at how something outside yourself (another person, object, or situation) seems to make you feel deficient in some way.

An Example of the Boomerang in Conjunction with the UI

In this example, Tricia is guided by a facilitator in following the steps outlined above.

Tricia: My husband, Brian, triggers me almost every day. I catch him looking at other women. I notice that he doesn't listen to me, and this really bothers me. I've tried talking to him about emotions, but he can't talk about them. He says I'm overreacting to everything.

Facilitator: In those moments when you catch him looking at other women, what does that mirror back to you about being deficient?

Tricia: Ugly. I feel like I'm not good enough for him.

Facilitator: How about the times when he isn't listening to you or doesn't want to talk about the things you wish to talk about?

Tricia: I feel as if he's shutting me out, and that hurts.

Facilitator: Now name the deficient self. If you could reduce that whole story about how he makes you feel to one specific kind of deficient self, what would it be? Reduce it down to something that really feels like you at the core.

Tricia: I'm not loved. That sums it up completely.

Facilitator: Now find it. Try to find that unloved self. Relax and just notice the capacity to be aware of thoughts coming and going. Look right at the words *I'm not loved.* Are those words you—the unloved self? If it helps, you can imagine putting those words in a picture frame in your mind, to really isolate them so you can look directly at them.

Tricia: Let me take a moment. Are the words *I'm not loved* me? Yes, that's me. That's how I feel about myself.

Facilitator: When words feel like who you are, it just means some emotion or sensation is arising along with the words. The words feel stuck to the emotion or sensation. That's the Velcro Effect. Take a moment, bring attention into your body, and see what emotion or sensation is arising.

Tricia: Sadness.

Facilitator: Look right at the word "sadness." Imagine the word in a picture frame. Is that you—the unloved self?

Tricia: No, that's clearly just a word.

Facilitator: Let that word fall away and bring attention back into your body. Can you feel the energy that you're calling sadness? Not the word "sadness," but the actual energy in your body?

Tricia: Yes.

Facilitator: Take a moment and just notice that you're presently aware of that energy, without a name for it. Gently observe that energy. Is that energy you—the unloved person?

Tricia: Yes, that's me.

Facilitator: Whenever an emotion or sensation feels like you, it just means there are some words or mental pictures arising along with it. If you just take a moment and look into your mind, watching thoughts, what words or pictures are arising along with that energy?

Tricia: The words *I've always had this problem with men.*

Facilitator: Look right at those words. Are those words you—the unloved self?

Tricia: Those are just words. When I looked at them, they fell away.

Facilitator: Bring attention back into your body. Do you feel that energy still?

Tricia: Yes.

Facilitator: Look again at that energy, without labeling it. Just let all words and pictures come to rest. Observe. Is that energy, by itself, you?

Tricia: No, that's just energy. And it dissolved as soon as those words dissolved.

Facilitator: Bring up a memory of the last time Brian wasn't listening to you and you felt hurt.

Tricia: That's not hard. He did it this morning.

Facilitator: Look directly at that mental picture of you talking this morning, while he's not listening. Frame it, if that helps. Is that picture you?

Tricia: No, that's just a memory. It's not me.

Facilitator: Look at the words *He looks at other women*. Are those words you—the unloved person? Stick to yes or no. Don't elaborate.

Tricia: No.

Facilitator: How about *He doesn't listen to me and this bothers me?*

Tricia: No.

Facilitator: Just be in presence for a few seconds, scanning the space of your inner body. Let any thought, emotion, or sensation arise naturally. Where's the unloved person? Can you find her?

Tricia: I don't know what you mean.

Facilitator: You've come to me saying that you're an unloved person. I assume that this is who you've taken yourself to be for many years, right?

Tricia: Yes, since childhood.

Facilitator: If this is really who you are, shouldn't you be able to find that right now? When a child is looking for an Easter egg, either she spots it or she doesn't. If there's an unloved person sitting with me here right now, can you point me to her?

Tricia: Yes, it's me.

Facilitator: Are the words *Yes, it's me* the unloved self?

Tricia: (*Laughing*) No! Just words.

Facilitator: Look for the unloved person.

Tricia: It seems to be in my name.

Facilitator: Look directly and only at the word "Tricia." Is that the unloved person?

Tricia: No, but it seems to point to her.

Facilitator: Find the unloved person who's right here. Not just words pointing to her. Find *her.*

Tricia: I can't. Wait, yes, I can. I see the thought *I know he loves me but I don't feel it.*

Facilitator: Are those words you, the unloved person? Don't think about the words or add more words to them. Just look directly at those words and answer.

Tricia: Well, intellectually, I know they're just words. But there's sadness arising again.

Facilitator: Whenever the body reacts to the words, just say yes. Bring your attention into the body to feel that energy without words and pictures. Is that energy you?

Tricia: No. The energy is going away now. It actually feels very warm and loving. I cannot find the unloved me at all. I'm now just sitting here in peace, feeling totally free of that story. I can see the memory of my dad now, though. He was cold. But when I look right at that picture, I can see it's not me, the unloved person. Wait, there's a picture in my mind of me as a ten-year-old girl. That's the unloved me.

Facilitator: Is that picture of the girl you, the unloved self?

Tricia: I can see it's just a picture. I went straight into the body to feel the energy of sadness and it washed through. No, it's not me. Wow, I've been in this story for a long time. I can't find her, the unloved self.

Facilitator: Take a look at Brian again in your mind. Does the sense that you're an unloved person arise when you look at him? Is the boomerang at work again?

Tricia: No, he looks perfect just as he is. I can see I love him. Actually, it's more than that. It's just love. I don't feel like it's missing. This was just a story I was placing on him. Thank you, thank you. This is as clear as day now. I feel so much lighter!

Facilitator: Yes, and when the story is "I'm unloved," we believe others contain our love, withholding it from us.

Tricia: What a cruel joke!

This is called the Boomerang because we bring these core deficiency stories to relationships. Like a boomerang, Tricia sent the message out that she feels like an unloved person. She played the part, spoke the language of an unloved person, and reacted to Brian from that belief about herself. Brian's actions were then interpreted by Tricia as unloving. Whether Brian's actions were objectively unloving makes no difference to Tricia's story. The interpretation was happening in Tricia's mind—in words, pictures, emotions, and sensations. The boomerang of "I'm unloved" came right back to Tricia.

There's an unconscious drive within us to attract people and situations and to interpret the actions of others in a way that confirms this core deficiency story. We solidify these stories over and over, like a pattern that repeats itself in all relationships, until that deficient self is seen through. Tricia was never a deficient person. There are no deficient people, just old scripts running.

Notice that, near the end, the facilitator asked Tricia to look again at Brian, once she couldn't find the unloved person. When she looked at him, she no longer felt that trigger. The deficient self did not arise. And so the interpretation of "I'm an unloved person" was no longer operating. That self was seen as "empty." The boomerang did not return.

Love feels natural once we stop telling the story "I am a separate, unloved person." Relationships automatically harmonize themselves once the deficient self is seen as unfindable. This doesn't mean we must stay in every relationship. We either stay or leave. The right action to take becomes clearer once we're no longer looking at others through the lens of a deficient self.

The Anxiety Inquiry

The last of the three Living Inquiries is the Anxiety Inquiry. Don't be fooled by the fact that I put it last in this series. Although it targets anxiety, it can be quite potent in releasing addictive cravings. This is because cravings are often accompanied by anxiety. Cravings and anxiety arise as one movement within the brain, working together to compel us toward addictive substances and activities. Once we are addicted, it feels as if using the addictive substance or activity is a matter of survival, and that feeling kicks in the fight-or-flight response. We are fleeing from our present experience, looking for something to medicate it or cover it up.

We may feel anxious around addiction for a number of other reasons beyond the anxiety that accompanies an urge. For example, anxiety can arise when we run out of our drug of choice or can't find a way to engage in our addictive activity. The fight-or-flight response kicks in during those moments too. There is also often a corresponding judgment that arises along with our cravings. For example, along with the thought *I want to swallow some painkillers*, there is sometimes an accompanying thought such as *I shouldn't*, or *I should quit painkillers*. We feel anxious about our addictions, as if there is an aversion that goes along with the addictions. Aversion actually fuels cravings. The more I think I shouldn't do something, the more I want to do it.

No matter what the source of the anxiety is, the Anxiety Inquiry (AI) can help.

Explanation of the Anxiety Inquiry

Let's keep this simple. The AI is just like the CI, except that we are looking for the threat in words, pictures, or energies (rather than looking for the command, as in the CI). Anxiety brings up the sense of an impending threat, real or imagined. Mostly it is imagined in our thoughts, causing us to feel discomfort or fear in our bodies. By "imagined," I mean we are not facing someone in the present moment pointing a gun at us, which would be a real threat to our physical survival. We are thinking about something. There is no real threat to our physical safety, but our minds and bodies don't know that. They react as if the threat is real.

Normally people use the word "threat" in the AI, but using the words "doom" or "danger" is fine too. In the AI, we isolate each element, slow it down, observe it, then ask the appropriate question toward each element: Is that picture the threat, are those words the threat, and is that energy the threat? In not finding a threat anywhere, and allowing each element to be as it is, the anxiety can fall away.

An Example of the Anxiety Inquiry

In this example, instead of having a facilitator take someone through the AI, I will explain how I might use the AI on my own. This will help you understand how to use it on your own, just as you can fly solo with any of the Inquiries. In the example below, I explain how to use the AI on several different forms of anxiety that arise along with cravings.

I notice that I am feeling anxious as I walk into a hotel with a bar in the lobby. The bar is stocked with every kind of alcohol you can imagine. My mouth starts watering. Anxiety is arising, along with a subtle craving in my stomach area. I could easily use the CI on this urge. But since there is anxiety present, I choose to use the AI.

I bring attention into the stomach area, noticing the peripheral space around the energy. I rest with it a bit, letting it float freely in that space. I ask, "Is that energy the threat?" The answer is yes because I notice a mental picture velcroed to the energy. The picture is of a glass of red wine. I slow that picture down, isolate it in my experience so that it is the only thing I am observing. I notice the peripheral space around the picture. I ask, "Is that picture the threat?" The picture begins to fade, as does the energy in my stomach, so the answer is no. It is no because there is no energy connected to the picture anymore.

I start walking to my hotel room. Before I open the door to the room, I feel a sense of lack, as if the night just won't be as good without a glass of wine. I hear the words *I'll be bored.* I then isolate those words, imagining them spelled out across the wall of the hotel room. I observe and rest with them for a bit. I then ask, "Are these words the threat?" The answer is yes because I feel that anxious energy in my stomach again. Remember, when looking at words or pictures, answer the question from the body. If you feel anything, it's a yes.

As the words slowly begin to disappear, I bring attention directly to that energy, while remaining aware of the peripheral space around it. I sit with it for a bit, just letting it be as it is. I feel some resistance, so I say to the energy, "Thank you for arising. I love you. Stay as long as you like." The resistance begins to fade. Then I ask, "Is that energy the threat?" The answer is no because I see no words or pictures. My mind is quiet. I allow the energy to be there, until it slowly dissolves away.

At first it feels as if the Inquiry is finished, so I turn on the TV for a bit. As I'm watching TV, I see a commercial for red wine. I feel a craving arise again, but this time I hear the words *You shouldn't drink wine. You've written a book about recovery. What would people think?* Ah, this sense of "I shouldn't" is a self-judgment (an aversion to wine), which then brings up anxiety again. This aversion actually fuels the craving. As I hear those words, I let them just be there in my awareness, without judgment, analysis, or commentary. I ask, "Are those words the threat?" The answer is yes, because the anxiety in my stomach is back. This time it is stronger than ever before. I feel some resistance to resting with it. I say to the energy again, "Thank you for arising. I love you. Stay as long as you like." The resistance begins to fade. I then ask, "Is there a threat in this energy?" The answer is no because there are no words or pictures arising with it. I allow the energy to be as it is until it fades away naturally. Now the Inquiry feels complete. No threat anywhere. I enjoy my night without any wine!

Weaving the CI and the AI Together

When you are experiencing cravings, you don't have to choose between the AI and the CI. You can weave them together. You can look for the command on certain words, pictures, and energies and weave in looking for the threat on others. Follow your intuition. It's fun to learn how to weave, but it takes time and practice. Play with it a little. If you need help, you know where to find a facilitator.

A Note About Trauma

Anxiety is sometimes connected to trauma. Trauma results from a previous pivotal event (or multiple events) in your life that was so scary or emotionally overwhelming that your system essentially shut down during or right after the event, so that you wouldn't have to feel the full effects of the emotional overwhelm. Unresolved trauma creates an imprint in your body and mind, such that you live in a continuous fight-or-flight response to life or experience an extreme fight-or-flight response in the face of triggers that are similar to the trigger in that previous event or events.

Trauma can result from events as extreme as rape or other forms of violence, but also from less obvious experiences, such as having an overly judgmental or protective parent. Trauma is unique to each individual and very subjective in nature. Two people can go through the same event and experience it very differently. One person will experience ongoing post-traumatic stress disorder (PTSD) or trauma after the event, while another person will seem unaffected to any great degree by the event.

Working with trauma on your own can be highly challenging. The fight-or-flight response can be so strong that you find yourself indulging in addictive substances and activities as a way to cope, unable to do the practices in this book. However, resolving trauma is key to recovery from addiction. Studies show that unresolved trauma is a major contributing factor in chronic relapsing.

If you believe you are experiencing trauma or PTSD and are medicating its effects with addictive substances, please contact the Kiloby Center at http://www.kilobycenter.com. We specialize in trauma work as it relates to addiction and chronic relapsing. If you cannot come to the Kiloby Center, work with a facilitator. The bodywork in chapter 7 can also help dissolve trauma.

Key Points

Here's a helpful review of the key concepts from this chapter:

The Compulsion Inquiry (CI). Use this Inquiry on any and all addictive substances and activities. Use the CI when there is any sense of *I have to, I must, I need to, I should,* craving, desire, or impulse. Example: Is this picture of heroin the command to use heroin? If you feel anything in the body, say yes and continue through the inquiry.

The Unfindable Inquiry (UI). Use this Inquiry on any deficiency stories or other false identities. Example: Are the words *I never get it right* the one who isn't good enough? Let your body answer, and then proceed through the inquiry.

The Boomerang. The Boomerang is a tool to help you see what others are mirroring back to you about who you think you are—usually a deficiency story. Example: What does my angry mother mirror back to me about who I am? *Ah, I'm the victim.* Then proceed through the UI looking for the victim.

The Anxiety Inquiry (AI). Use this Inquiry whenever you sense a threat in your experience that creates anxiety or fear (usually about the future). This includes when you hear the mind projecting words or pictures that indicate the need to protect or defend, be safe, hide, avoid, hold back, resist, get angry, become irritated, fight, flee, attack, become numb, or shut down. Example: Is this picture of being homeless a threat? Again, if there is any feeling or sensation, say yes and then proceed through the inquiry.

Helpful hints. In the section of this chapter on the Unfindable Inquiry, you read a subsection called "A Few Helpful Tips." Many of those tips are also helpful when learning and practicing the CI and AI. Study them carefully.

CHAPTER 7

Dissolving Body Contractions

The topic of dissolving body contractions deserves its own chapter. In fact, it probably deserves its own book. In my view, it is critically important to addiction recovery.

What are body contractions? They are blockages of energy (sometimes repressed emotion) in various parts of the inner body that feel denser than other sensations. For example, have you ever felt emotion well up inside you only to get stuck in the throat area, as if you cannot truly express the emotion? That's a *contraction*. Another example is the stomach area. When you feel highly anxious or stressed out, notice how your stomach feels a bit like a clenched fist. That's a contraction. Many also experience a contraction in the heart area. For example, clients at the Kiloby Center coming off heroin often experience a strong blockage of energy in the heart. I call this the Heroin Heart.

Blockages can be anywhere in the body, but they tend to show up mostly in the root (base of the spine), pelvis, stomach, sternum, heart, throat, and head—aligning with the chakra system from certain Eastern spiritual traditions. Many people, when first starting presence work, are not even aware that they carry such blockages. They are not yet fully tuned into the inner awareness of their bodies at that deeper level. But these blockages play a central role in addiction, trauma, depression, and anxiety, even if we don't realize it. It is only when these blockages dissolve that we begin to truly realize how deeply they have affected behaviors and well-being. For example, when a client at the Center experiences the dissolving of the Heroin Heart, there is immense relief and often a great reduction or elimination of all cravings for heroin and other opiates.

It's important to share my personal experience here. I was an opiate addict. After a number of months practicing the tools in this book, I experienced a tremendous opening of the contraction in my heart. This came after resting with the blocked energy in my heart on a daily basis. It's as if my heart literally burst open with energy dispersing in every direction, leaving only a feeling of love and peace in that area. As a result, my cravings for opiates vanished. Later in my journey, I began to notice a blockage in my throat area. All my life I had trouble expressing myself and my emotions. The practices here dissolved that throat blockage. The throat then felt empty and transparent. I began to express myself much more freely. The addictions connected to that area—tobacco and sweets— dissolved. I had similar experiences in my sternum, stomach, and pelvic area, with the falling away of addictions connected to those spots.

You may ask, "Why do addictions fall away as these blockages dissolve?" I'm afraid that we just don't have the answer quite yet. Science has not caught up with the experience of those using meditation and mindfulness in very transformative ways. Perhaps one day we will have a sufficient scientific answer. For now, I ask you to trust me: these blockages are directly connected to addictions. I've seen it in my own experience and the experience of countless others with whom I have worked.

The reason for this connection could be that these blockages often contain repressed emotion, and addiction is all about repressing emotion, as we continuously stuff down our feelings with substances and activities. As the repressed emotion releases, the addictions release. Contractions may be connected to unresolved trauma. In many of the private sessions I have done with people at the Kiloby Center, the dissolving of a certain blockage has brought about a corresponding relief from long-held trauma. For many people, unresolved trauma is one of the major contributing factors in addiction and chronic relapse.

It could be that these blockages are connected to our basic sense of separation, discussed in "The Living Inquiries" chapter. We feel energetically and physically separate from each other and from life, in part because of the body being experienced as contracted and separate. This contracted experience of the body (the trauma of being a human thrust into a world of separation, if you will) leads us to fight for our individual survival. Addiction is all about survival. The same mechanism that drives us toward food for physical survival kicks in when we are addicted to substances and activities not directly linked to physical survival. Imagine the first humans, needing to survive in the most fundamental way on a daily basis. How would they have found the motivation to return to the berries or hunt down animals for food without that clenching sensation in their bodies compelling them again and again toward these things? Addiction to substances and activities is closely associated with that visceral need to survive. In the moment when you want a cigarette, it can feel as if you won't survive without it (even when you rationally know that this isn't true). You *have* to have it! Your body carries a physical drive that practically screams for a smoke. That's the contraction screaming.

Connecting Addictions to Certain Body Contractions

Regardless of the theories presented, the important thing to remember is that these contractions can be dissolved, and their release can bring about a tremendous reduction or elimination of addictive cravings. If you are wondering which body contractions tend to be tied to which addictions, I have provided the following list as a guide. It is merely a guide, based on my own experience and the experience of the thousands of people with whom I have done the kind of deep bodywork discussed later in this chapter.

Root area (located at the base of the spine). This area is connected to issues around safety and security. Blockage in this area is associated with addictions to money, security, safety, food, gambling, shopping, work, heroin, cocaine, alcohol, milk, fat, meats, and benzos (Valium and Xanax).

Pelvic area (located in the pelvic region, just above the genitals). This area involves mainly emotion and sexuality. Blockages here are associated with addictions to alcohol, heroin, painkillers, sex, porn, gluten, wheat, starchy carbs, grain-based alcohol, and chocolate.

Stomach area (located in the midstomach and sometimes affects the whole stomach area, including the sternum area). This area is connected to personal will, drive, and self-identity. Contractions here are associated with addictions to speed, meth, cocaine, caffeine, work, sex, anger, cannabis, carbonated beverages, corn-based alcohol, beer, corn-processed sugars, other foods, and benzos.

Heart area (located in the chest and connected to the throat). It involves mainly love, compassion, and openness or lack thereof. Those with a blockage in this area may experience addictions to tobacco (smoking, because it involves lungs), sugar, love, marijuana, ecstasy, smoking, wine and the other sugary alcohols, opiates (all forms, including heroin and pain-killers), and benzos.

Throat area (located at the base of the throat and extending up through the throat to the mouth area). This area is connected to creativity and self-expression or an inability to express oneself. It is associated with addictions to marijuana, opiates, food, tobacco (smoking and chew), and other oral fixations or addictions.

Mind's eye area (located in the forehead). It involves mainly thinking and cognition. Blockages here are associated with addictions to thinking, over-intellectualizing, hallucinogens, marijuana, chocolate, caffeine, and most mood-altering substances and activities.

Crown area (located at the top of the head). It involves religion, spiritual seeking, and other goals related to higher or transcendent states. Blockages here are associated with addictions to spiritual seeking or religious beliefs and most mind-altering substances and activities.

Last, but certainly not least, is the Kiloby Clearing Method. This one is my favorite. Hence, it has my name on it. What I have come to see with the various inquiries and methods I've developed through the years is that there isn't one size that fits all. People resonate with different inquiries and methods. The Kiloby Clearing Method just happens to be the one that has helped me the most with regard to clearing bodily blockages and contractions and dissolving the addictions and traumas that are associated with them. I've also found it to work very effectively and efficiently with many clients at the Kiloby Center.

Sit or lie quietly, using the breathing exercises mentioned above in order to relax and become aware of your inner body. Feel into the area that seems tight, contracted, or blocked. Rest there for a bit—thirty seconds or so.

After feeling into that area, close your eyes and rotate your eyeballs to the left of your body—directly *outside* of the body and to the immediate left of the area where the blockage or contraction is. As you rotate your eyeballs to the left side, become aware of the space to the left of the area of the body. Notice any words, images, or memories in that space.

Now take two fingers and begin tapping continuously on your forehead right above the bridge of your nose. As you tap, pull up with your awareness each set of words, each image, and each memory—one by one—into the tapping area. Your eyeballs will move from the left side of the body to the tapping area as you do this. Once the set of words, image, or memory is brought into the tapping area, immediately start focusing only on the tapping sensation. This exercise is a lot like dragging and dropping a file on your computer. But in this case you are dragging these thoughts, one by one, and dropping them into the tapping area. This helps to disconnect you from the thoughts that are embedded in the contracted area of your body.

Continue bringing up sets of words, images, and memories—one by one—into the tapping area in this way, always changing your focus to the tapping once the thought has been brought into the tapping area. Do this until there are no more words, images, or memories in that space to the left side of your body.

Now, feel into the sensation that was previously contracted or tight. It should feel lighter. Rest with your attention right on top of the sensation if it is still there. If the sensation moves or changes in any way, move your attention so that it is resting on the top of the sensation no matter where the sensation goes or how it changes. It's important to continuously keep your attention resting right on top of the sensation. By "top," I mean the side of the sensation closest to the sky, if you are standing up or sitting up in a chair. This helps to bring the energy up and out of your spine. Continue resting on top of the sensation until the blockage is clear.

If the blockage or contraction remains, go back to the first part of the exercise involving the tapping, then return to resting on top, and continue alternating between these two exercises. It is important to be thorough while doing the exercises. This exercise takes patience. Spend a good deal of time doing this exercise every day—at least an hour a day.

As you use the tools in this book, including the Living Inquiries, you are likely to bump into these contractions in your body. If you do, then take care to notice any connections between certain blockages and the addictions you experience, as listed above.

Notice also that addiction is often about substitution. For example, as soon as you drop your addiction to alcohol, you may find yourself overindulging in sweets. If you drop caffeine, you may find yourself feeling addicted to work. The reason for this substitution is that the blockage in that particular area has not yet dissolved. It's still screaming for something. When you take away one of its addictions, a substitution takes its place.

Holding Back the Dam

Many people recovering from drug and alcohol addiction are holding back the dam. Holding back the dam is like living your life on the brink of relapse, as if at any given moment you could spiral right back down into drug and alcohol addiction. One way we hold back the dam is to substitute one addiction for another. We haven't quite dealt with the underlying issues, so we are in survival mode, trying as best we can to keep ourselves from taking that drink while scarfing down cookies to satisfy those strong bodily urges.

Holding back the dam happens when we do not fully face and dissolve the body contractions discussed in this chapter. Without doing that work, we are merely refraining from using—that's all. The potential for relapse is still there as a real possibility because of these unresolved aspects of our experience. Our bodies continue to cry out for relief of some kind.

When these contractions dissolve, we are no longer holding back the dam. Our bodies feel better and lighter. There is no longer a clenched fist in the stomach, a closed heart, or a lumpy throat. Therefore, we no longer need various addictions to medicate these areas. The dam bursts open, allowing a new way of being in the world, without enslavement to addiction and its corresponding game of substitution.

Mapping Out the Tools

Before I give you some tools to help dissolve contractions, I want to provide a map for how to use the various tools in this book at different stages of your recovery and explain how and why bodywork is like the final frontier in the Natural Rest way of recovery. I chose to provide this map at this later point in the book for a reason. Had I provided it in the beginning, you would not have had a chance to use the other tools first. This book progresses deeper and deeper into experience. By now, you have some experience using the Living Inquiries and with resting and allowing all words, pictures, and energies to come and go within awareness. Being able to use these tools is critical for bodywork. Bodywork includes all of them.

Take a look at this diagram:

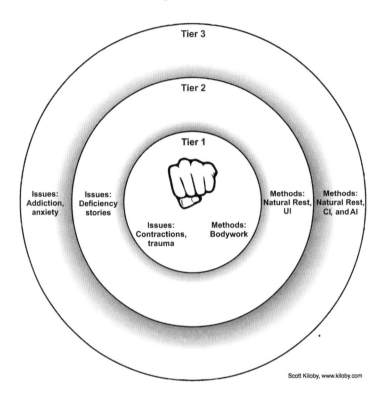

Scott Kiloby, www.kiloby.com

Notice the three tiers of experience: Tier 1, Tier 2, and Tier 3. These tiers denote the various depths to which you can take the tools in this book. They also denote layers of experience.

On the outer layer, Tier 3, we experience surface-level behaviors like addiction and its accompanying anxiety. If necessary, return to the chapter on the Living Inquiries and read about the connection between addiction and anxiety to refresh your memory. Putting to rest these behaviors in Tier 3 is often about simply choosing to stop smoking one day or going into a detox center to get off drugs and alcohol. The basic tools in chapters 1 through 3 as well as the Compulsion and Anxiety Inquiries in chapter 6 can be very helpful in stopping these behaviors. Tier 3 behaviors are the outer manifestation of Tier 1 and 2 issues. It is often said in 12-step rooms, "Drugs are not the problem; they are the symptoms." Merely stopping a behavior does not deal with these Tier 1 and 2 issues. We have to go deeper into our experience to truly address those issues. Without going deeper, we remain highly prone to relapse and substitution. We are holding back the dam.

True recovery is not about stopping. It's about doing the work necessary so that a true transformation is experienced, one that provides deep assurances that you will not fall back into the addictive cycle. This first takes us to Tier 2, which is about dealing with the deficiency stories and other false identities that contribute to medicating, covering up, or escaping the uncomfortable or painful feelings that accompany these stories. The Unfindable Inquiry in chapter 6 is particularly helpful in this area.

Tier 1 involves entering the deeper layer of experience— body contractions. Even when we begin to see through the deficiency and other false stories we have been carrying around for years, our bodies may still scream for relief through addictive substances and activities. At the level of survival, there is still a physical urge to reach for these things, even if those urges quieted a bit through Inquiry work.

In the remaining section of this chapter, I provide tools to enter into this deeper layer, to dissolve these contractions, and to end the phenomenon of holding back the dam when it comes to the physical nature of addiction.

Beginning Bodywork

Let's move to bodywork, now that you have a better context for why it is so important. Notice where your addictions are connected to certain areas of the body. Review the list above explaining these connections. Let's call this the target area. You may find more than one target area. That's quite common. In doing bodywork, the key is to focus on the area that seems more contracted or most at the forefront of your awareness.

If you have difficulty locating the target area, use the hose metaphor: While sitting quietly, imagine a hose running from the top of your head to the bottom of your groin. As you breathe in and allow the air to flow all the way down your body, notice any kinks in the hose. These are areas where the air doesn't seem to flow directly down. The air seems to go around or bypass certain blocked areas. Those kinks are contractions. Contractions tend to be located in front of the spine (and sometimes anchored to the spine and extending outward from it). For example, a heart contraction may appear as a sensation in the middle of your chest. But you may notice as you explore it more deeply that it feels anchored to the spine.

As you feel into that area, notice how it feels different from other areas of the body. For example, compared to the arm, your stomach may feel very tight. Once you have located the contraction (the target area you want to work with), explore each of the exercises below until you find one or a combination of several that work well for you. Then use those practices every day, for at least an hour per day.

The key to all these exercises is patience. Do not look for quick results. Do not look for any results. Have no expectations.

Instead, just be curious and explore within the natural rest of presence. The dissolving of contractions happens on its own time, in its own way. And most of all, as peculiar as this sounds, don't get caught up in the trap of *trying* to dissolve these contractions. When you are trying, you are often resisting the contractions by trying to get them to dissolve. This actually adds resistance to the contractions, which makes them stay.

Instead, let resting in the spaciousness of the present moment be the foundation for these exercises. You aren't going anywhere. You aren't trying to get to a later moment when all contractions have dissolved. That's seeking. Instead, just rest. The more you gently allow and explore within the natural rest of presence, the more you give these contractions permission and space to dissolve on their own. That's what I mean by infinite patience. This moment is an infinite space. Be patient within that space and come back to these exercises often with childlike, gentle curiosity.

The Exercises

Before you begin any one of these exercises, get quiet and relaxed first. Sit or lie down in a quiet place away from everyone and everything. Begin breathing in and out through your nostrils with long, slow breaths. As you inhale, bring attention into the contraction. As you exhale, notice how the exhalation reveals spaciousness around the contraction. Notice the space inside and around your whole body as one undivided space. Continue breathing in this way until you sense your mind quieting much more. Then, begin the exercise. While doing any of the exercises below, it is important to be peripherally aware of the space inside the contraction and all around it. After all, when it dissolves, it will dissolve into that space. Remaining aware of that space helps the dissolving take place.

Bodywork is, of course, all about the body. But the body is connected to the mind. The Velcro Effect explains this. Emotions and sensations are often stuck, or velcroed, to certain words and pictures. Therefore, while doing bodywork, remain aware of any words or pictures that arise and deal with them through witnessing or inquiry. If any words or pictures arise, observe them gently, let them be there until they dissolve away naturally, then move back to the contraction and continue exploring it with one or more of the exercises below.

Metaphysical Hands

The first exercise is called Metaphysical Hands. Contractions stick around because of conscious or unconscious resistance to them. We spend our whole lives keeping them in place in various ways, including by acting out with addictive substances and activities as a way to avoid truly facing and feeling them. Metaphysical Hands is a way of quieting down all that resistance. As resistance fades, contractions are able to expand, move, and dissolve more easily.

Imagine two hands (not your real hands) embracing the contraction, cupping it on each side, and holding it in place. See if you can keep the contraction the same size and in the same location just by holding it with these imaginary hands. As this quiets the resistance to the contraction, you may start to feel it move. It may change locations or change its size—getting bigger or smaller. Whatever happens, allow those imaginary hands to follow the contraction. If it moves to a different location, imagine the hands cupping and holding it at the new location. If it changes size, allow the hands to cup and hold the contraction in its new size. Continue doing this until the contraction fades or dissolves.

Making It Stay

As stated above, the intention to make a contraction go away is resistance. Just as the Metaphysical Hands exercise helps to relax the resistance, Making It Stay helps also, which in turn helps the dissolving of the contraction.

First, become aware of your desire for the contraction in the target area to dissolve. Gently observe that desire, however it shows up (in words or otherwise), until that desire begins to fade and you are resting in the present space allowing the contraction to just be as it is.

Bring attention into the contraction, feeling all the way into it. See if you can make it stay *just* by feeling it, nothing else. Of course, you can't. That's the key. This practice of making the contraction stay just by feeling it (and being aware of the space around it) reverses that desire to make it go away. It's like loving the contraction to death by actually wanting it to remain there. It's a deep acceptance of the contraction as it is, which often helps to give it the space to dissolve finally. Again, it's all about infinite patience. The contraction may not dissolve. But at least you are accepting it as it is—loving it, even. This is much more effective than trying to get rid of it, which often just creates more resistance.

Find the Pinpoint Within

One night before falling asleep, I began to bring my attention to a long-held pain in front of my spine (right above my sternum) that, as a result of some tainted ecstasy I took at age twenty, had negatively affected my quality of life for years. This spinal pain was like a contraction, and it was connected to certain addictive urges. I felt into a pinpoint in the middle of the pain and just rested my attention there for about thirty minutes. Suddenly, the blockage dissolved into what felt like an electrical storm throughout my body. This was a very pleasant relief. When I woke up the next day, the pain was gone. I felt tremendous freedom from the pain. It never returned.

Finding the pinpoint within involves first recognizing that there is no real pinpoint. It's not like every contracted target area has a clear nucleus or center. The key is to bring attention into what you feel to be the very center of the contraction, pinpointing your attention right there and then keeping and resting your attention there for a long period of time. As stated above, you may see words and pictures arising out of the contraction. If so, simply witness them gently, allow them to be, and allow them to dissolve on their own. Then come back to resting attention in the pinpoint of the contraction. This exercise may or may not help. Just try it. And don't expect an electrical storm or release like I had. Have no expectations. Just try the exercise and move on if it doesn't help.

Mining

Mining is a process by which you literally mine out certain words or pictures that are embedded in (or velcroed to) the contraction. When first resting with a contraction, it is not always easy to see what words and pictures are connected to it. It can seem as if you are just sitting with a body sensation by itself, but the sensation feels stuck because there are unconscious words or pictures associated with it.

With Mining, you are pulling out each set of words and each picture, one by one. The following questions can help pull out this unconscious material. Use one or more of these questions when you sense that there are words or pictures connected with the target area but you aren't quite aware of them yet. These are called elicitation questions:

What's really going on here?

What's the worst that can happen?

What does this contraction mean?

What am I really afraid of?

What am I holding onto?

What does this blockage represent?

What do I really want?

What do I want to do with this?

What's the best that can happen?

What if this never leaves?

What goes with this sensation?

Once you ask one or more of the questions, sit quietly and watch for anything that arises in the form of words or pictures. When you see something, witness it gently, allow it to be in the open space, and allow it to dissolve on its own naturally. You may experience a flood of words and pictures as a result of asking one of the questions. Isolate each set of words and each picture in the flood. Let each set of words and each picture dissolve away on its own. Then return to exploring the target area in the body and returning to the question(s) when necessary. Some people see sensations as having a certain form or shape. For example, a throat contraction may appear to awareness as an egg shape. You can isolate such shapes, witness them as you would witness any picture, and allow them to dissolve one by one.

As an alternative to witnessing and allowing, you can use the Inquiries you learned in chapter 6. For example, suppose you feel a contraction in your stomach area and you have a sense that it is based in fear but you aren't aware of any words or pictures. You might use the elicitation question "What am I really afraid of?" Once you ask the question, you see a picture of yourself as homeless and living on the streets as a result of not being able to pay bills, along with some other words and pictures. Look at each picture, one by one, asking, "Is that the threat?" Do the same with each set of words. When the words and pictures dissolve away, return to feeling into the stomach contraction. Continue Mining.

Once you have mined out everything contained in a contraction, it tends to dissolve. It may not dissolve completely the first few times you use the Mining process. But as you continue to use it, you should find great relief from the contraction.

If you have any difficulty with mining, I suggest working with a trained facilitator, who can help you with the process. Visit http://www.livinginquiries.com.

The NOW Method

Some find the NOW Method to be helpful with regard to contractions. NOW stands for *notice, open, watch*. Here's how it works:

Notice the contraction. Locate it with awareness and begin feeling it directly, without words and pictures on it.

Open to the space around it. Open your attention to the peripheral space around the feeling, and allow the sensation to float freely in that open space.

Watch for any movement of fight or flight. Fight movements can appear as words, like *I don't want to feel this*, or other words or pictures that tend to be associated with wanting the contraction to change or go away. Fight movements also include any other form of resistance to the contraction that you feel in the body. Flight movements include words or pictures having to do with wanting to escape or turn away from the contraction. Just become aware of these movements. Allow them to arise in awareness and be as they are. When you remain aware of them, they tend to dissolve, allowing you to be with the actual contraction more easily. As you are resting and feeling into the contraction without any fight or flight movements, the contraction is being accepted as it is and given permission to dissolve away.

Key Points

Here's a brief review of the main points about dissolving body contractions:

Locate the contraction (the target area). Use the metaphor of the hose running from the top of your head to the bottom of your groin. As you breathe in and allow the air to flow all the way down your body, notice any kinks in the hose. Those kinks are contractions.

Prepare for bodywork. Begin breathing in and out through your nostrils with long, slow breaths. As you inhale, bring attention into the contraction. As you exhale, notice how the exhalation reveals spaciousness around the contraction.

Use one of the bodywork exercises above. Find one (or more) exercise that works well for you. Practice it daily, for at least an hour a day in a quiet place. Remember: Infinite patience.

CHAPTER 8

Misconceptions and Traps

A misconception is essentially any mistaken view or attitude. Several of the misconceptions discussed in this chapter arise from overintellectualizing, rather than taking up the practice of actually resting in presence.

There's a simple sweetness and well-being available to you through the practice of resting in presence. It's something that can never be experienced merely through emphasizing beliefs or opinions about presence or about this way of recovery.

When we fully commit without reservation to the practice of resting in presence throughout the day, whenever possible, this sweetness and well-being become available to us.

This way of recovery is too simple and obvious to comprehend through the mind. When we try to figure it out with the mind and emphasize viewpoints about where we are on a time-bound path, we stay locked in self-centeredness and personal seeking. We miss the treasure available to us in restful presence.

Traps are places where we get stuck. By discussing these traps in this chapter, it may be easier to see them if they arise. In seeing them, we begin to be free of them.

Not everyone involved in this way of recovery will experience these misconceptions and traps. If any of these things arise for you, just revisit this chapter.

Lack of Readiness

Readiness is an attitude of openness and willingness to get clean and sober, as well as to use the tools in this book to really uproot and dissolve the issues connected to addiction.

It takes a great degree of readiness, for example, to check oneself into a detox unit or participate in the Kiloby Center's program, where we teach and practice these tools every day. It also takes a great degree of readiness to pick up the practices in this book and use them diligently at home.

Our systems are designed to want to cover up, escape, or run from anything painful. It can be painful, at first, to begin truly facing the pain we have been trying to escape for years. I can assure you that doing this work has tremendous rewards. I've never seen a person dive deeply into this work only to regret it later.

But the harsh reality is that not everyone is ready to take these steps. Sometimes we have to hit rock bottom to become fully ready. Not everyone has to hit such a bottom. Some become open and willing simply because they are sick and tired of living in the enslavement of addiction. The point is this: using this program of recovery absolutely requires readiness.

If you are struggling with readiness, I suggest doing a few sessions with a trained facilitator. A facilitator can guide you through the Anxiety Inquiry and other Inquiries to help you face, uproot, and dissolve fears or anxieties you may have regarding stopping the use of certain substances and activities, or beginning the practices in this book.

Measuring Progress

Before coming to the practice of presence, we lived with the habitual tendency to look to thoughts of the past and future for a sense of self. We consulted the past story to know who we are and emphasized the story of the future to know who we are becoming.

It makes perfect sense, *at first,* to treat recovery through presence the same way. We may find ourselves measuring back in time, saying things like "I'm much more present than I was a year ago, and I feel like I will learn to be even more present in the future." Again, at first, this is fine. It may actually empower us to continue making restful presence the most important thing in our lives.

But through resting in presence, we come to see that this measuring backward and forward is just more self-centeredness.

By noticing any thoughts that arise in some attempt to measure backward or forward in time, we take a moment to rest in presence. Present rest doesn't depend on anything that happened in the past. It also has nothing to do with any future moments of rest. To look to the future is to seek, even if we're looking for more rest in the future.

All sorts of interesting and profound spiritual experiences and states *may* arise through the practice of resting in presence. These experiences and states aren't a necessary part of recognizing presence, but they may accompany it. Some people experience them, some don't.

Past states and experiences are nothing more than memories appearing within presence. Future expectations about spiritual experiences and states are also nothing more than thoughts arising now.

Profound spiritual experiences and states aren't the goal here. States and experiences, no matter how positive or negative, are seen to be equal energies of presence. We enjoy positive experiences and states, but we don't emphasize them for a sense of self.

The real power of natural rest lies in recognizing selfless presence as the stable, unchanging space in which all experiences, states, and other energies come and go freely.

This reveals to us incredible freedom and equanimity.

In restful presence, we see that measuring our progress in time simply isn't needed anymore. It becomes irrelevant. The sacredness of life is always here now.

Selfless presence carries a well-being that's never dependent on what happened before or what might happen later.

Mistaking Presence for Amnesia

It's a misconception to believe that presence is like amnesia. We don't lose our memories in presence.

Our stories remain fully available to us even once we see that these stories are not who we ultimately are. We continue to have a conventional self. A conventional self is not a real, separate, permanent, objective self. That kind of self is unfindable. A conventional self is a play of ever-changing words, pictures, and energy coming and going in the present moment. We don't deny these appearances coming and going. We just see that they never form anything real, separate, permanent, or objective. We continue to use our names, remember our pasts, and have thoughts about the future. This way of recovery is about no longer *identifying* with these thoughts. It's not about getting rid of them or forgetting things about our personal histories.

Mistaking Presence for Escape

In first hearing of the practice of resting in presence and letting all energies come and go equally without emphasizing any of them, it may sound as if we're trying to escape life or whatever's appearing in life. This is a misconception, which usually comes from *thinking* about presence rather than the practice of resting in presence itself.

Let's take fear as an example. Whenever fear arises, it almost always relates to self-centered thought. The thoughts that accompany the fear refer to a self that feels threatened in some way. Whether we're thinking about an upcoming speech we have to give at work or knee replacement surgery, *it's all the same*. Fear keeps us trapped in a self-centered story.

This story doesn't really face anything. It tries to run away.

In this story, thought is working hard to cover up, get rid of, neutralize, or rationalize the fear. Thought plays out future scenarios, desperately looking for the scenario that says, "Everything will be okay." This is all an attempt to make the presently arising fear go away. This is the very definition of escape.

In presence, we're facing the suffering directly. We're looking at the thoughts that make up the story, seeing them for what they are—just thoughts arising and falling in restful presence. By bringing attention into the body where the raw energy of fear is arising, we're finally facing this fear that has been running our lives and fueling these thoughts.

In presence, we're not escaping things. We're facing them. We're seeing that each word, picture, and energy is a temporary appearance only. Through presence, we're released from the drive to escape whatever's happening to us.

Although fear is being used as an example here, this applies to every thought, emotion, and sensation.

To face a thought or emotion doesn't mean to apply pressure toward it. It means to have no agenda about the thought or emotion. It means to have no desire to escape anything that arises. It means to allow all arisings to be exactly as they are, while resting in presence. This is about complete nonresistance to all energies, no matter what form they take.

When we turn to face what's arising, we find these energies aren't the big, bad monsters we thought they were. We find that presence is not in opposition to anything that arises. In this seeing, we discover that there's no self at the center of life.

All energies are seen to be equal movements of this selfless presence. In this seeing, the escaping stops.

Substitution

Substitution is a common trap. It is the act of replacing one addictive substance or activity for another.

Here's an example:

Jill is addicted to meth but there are times when the drug isn't available. So she substitutes alcohol or pills.

There are also times when she tries to get clean on her own, without the help of any program. She goes for months at a time abstaining from drugs and alcohol completely. But during these abstinent periods, she finds herself preoccupied and even obsessed with issues surrounding weight loss, work, and boyfriends. She's again substituting.

After a period of abstinence from drugs and alcohol, Jill picks up meth again. She gets arrested and then placed in jail. While sitting in jail, she obsesses over her past and constantly thinks about what will happen to her in the future. She's substituting again. This time her drug of choice is excessive thinking.

After being released from jail, Jill decides to get involved in a recovery program. In this program, she finds freedom from her desire to use drugs and alcohol, but she also finds herself obsessed with money and shopping. Again, she's substituting. She works through those issues, and then she becomes preoccupied with seeking self-improvement and spiritual awakening in the future. Another substitution.

To the mind, the content doesn't matter. Thought will obsess over any substance or activity, including seeking spiritual awakening.

Although some substances or activities seem to be more addictive than others, when we look more closely, all addiction arises from the same Velcro Effect of words, pictures, and energies feeling stuck together. No matter how much or how often we substitute one substance or activity for another, the structure's always the same. We're locked in a search for something else, something more.

In treating all substances and activities as equal, we are never disqualified from recovery. Natural rest helps release us from any and all addictions. We find no need to reach for a substitute when the seeking energy behind all addictions relaxes.

Confusing Pleasure with Addiction and Compulsion

It may seem as if the goal of this way of recovery is to rid ourselves of the enjoyment of pleasure. But enjoying life's pleasures itself is not addiction.

Addiction is a repetitive, compulsive need for a particular substance or activity. For example, those who are not addicted to chocolate can eat it every now and then. They can *truly* take it or leave it! It's not a compulsion. They do not obsess over it. They do not have to have it every day or on some other repeated basis. They do not use it to medicate painful emotions. They simple enjoy it, moderately.

Compulsion is quite different. It's the sense of *having to have* a particular substance or engage in a particular activity, usually on a repeated basis (sometimes through bingeing). Addiction and compulsion are ways of trying to medicate painful feelings, escape a continuous sense of boredom or restlessness, or quiet excited or anxious thoughts or emotions.

When there is a compulsion, we cannot simply "take or leave" that substance or activity. We *have* to have it! Seeing the difference between addiction and the simple, occasional enjoyment of life's pleasures is critical to a healthy view of recovery.

Whatever you do, don't fool yourself! Recognize a compulsion for what it is. Notice when you can't just take or leave a substance or activity. That's a compulsion.

Release the whole movement of compulsion itself using the practices and inquiries in this book. Let that be your first priority.

Don't deceive yourself into thinking that you are merely enjoying beer in the way that others enjoy an occasional brownie. Can you take or leave the beer? Are you using caffeine, drugs, food, or shopping to medicate feelings? That's the key to knowing whether there is an addiction present. If there is no compulsion, you should be able to enjoy certain pleasures in life with a take it or leave it attitude. Anything else is addiction.

Turning Natural Rest into Busywork

Busywork is a trap related to substitution, but it deserves its own discussion. In several chapters of this book, you'll find sets of inquiries and exercises. These practices help us question the thoughts that keep us locked in the cycle of replaying the past and seeking the future.

None of these practices are meant to keep us busy thinking about ourselves all the time. They are about selfless presence, which is *freedom from the habitual tendency to focus on the self.*

The Inquiries and the other tools in this book are designed to assist us in resting in presence on an ongoing basis. That's it! They're not designed to get us trapped in the cycle of seeking a better version of ourselves in the future or obsessing over busy spiritual work.

In this way of recovery, we're only interested in present rest. If a spiritual practice isn't designed to awaken us to this moment, where freedom really is, it's probably just keeping us asleep within our self-centered story.

Viewing Compatible Practices as Incompatible

It may seem at first that resting in thought-free presence is incompatible with allowing all energies, including thoughts, to come and go freely.

In resting in thought-free presence, our aim isn't to suppress, destroy, or get rid of thought. We see that our real identity isn't any of the temporary thoughts or other energies that appear and disappear within the thought-free presence.

Through resting in the natural rest of the present moment, we come to see that thought arises spontaneously and involuntarily. If, at any moment, we believe we have control over thoughts and other energies, then all we have to do is ask: "Do I know what energy movement will arise next? Do I know what my next thought will be?"

There's no way to know what thought or other energy movement will appear until it's already appeared. By that time, if we don't emphasize it and simply let it be as it is, we see that it's already on its way to disappearing. All energies are equal. They all do this. They arise spontaneously and involuntarily. They hang around for a while, and then disappear. When we make resting in presence the most important thing in our lives, none of these energies leave any trace.

Thoughts and all other energies are allowed to be just as they are. We no longer try to control this flow of energy.

We see that the natural rest of presence is the space in which all energies come and go. We see that resting in presence is perfectly compatible with allowing all energies to be as they are.

Story Mind vs. Functional Mind

Another viewpoint that can arise is the belief that presence will render us unable to function. We may believe that presence means we become dumb and unable to perform even simple life tasks.

This is a misconception. Again, it comes from emphasizing ideas about what presence might look like instead of actually taking up the practice of repeatedly resting in presence.

Through resting in presence, the self-centered story is seen through. The addictive cycle of personal seeking falls away. Thoughts are seen to be transparent. We're no longer identified with them. Functioning, however, continues perfectly.

To shed some light on this misconception, it may be helpful to make a distinction between story mind and functional mind.

In story mind, we're constantly seeking to gain something personally from the future, others, and situations. We act from a sense of lack or try to escape past negative feelings. We act from within a story, trying to control outcomes. In this story, the present moment is overlooked in favor of thoughts about the past and future. This stifles our ability to function effectively and with a clear mind.

In functional mind, we live and act from selfless presence. We're not looking to gain anything personally. We don't need anything. This moment contains perfect completeness.

Yet movement and functioning unfold intuitively within the stillness of presence, without a need to control outcomes. We find that all energies and movement arise spontaneously, causelessly, and dynamically as part of the natural flow of life. Whether we're talking to a friend, driving a car, or studying quantum physics, functioning happens effortlessly and effectively in presence.

We don't become perfect human beings. We see there's no such thing. Perfect functioning means living in the present moment without emphasizing the story that life should be the way we want it to be, or should unfold the way we believe it should unfold.

We see that the ideal of a perfect person was being sought only because we saw ourselves as deficient at the core. That false belief is seen through with the Unfindable Inquiry (and the Boomerang). We function more freely without that belief and the impossible standard it carries with it.

Unique Struggles

As soon as they begin this way of recovery, some may find it very easy to rest in presence. Some may struggle at first and then find it easier once they stop being so hard on themselves.

If there's an initial struggle, it may be easier to take only very brief moments of rest many times throughout the day. The moments eventually become longer. Then at some point, there will be a natural return to presence that requires little to no effort.

Others may struggle against resting in presence for a more substantial period of time. The inability to rest in presence almost always comes from the habitual tendency to emphasize thoughts. These thoughts are often about (1) how the past was better or worse than the present moment, (2) how the present moment isn't the way it's supposed to be, or (3) how the future will be better or worse.

It may be helpful to write out all these thoughts that are coming up regularly, that are making it difficult to rest. By putting them on paper, we may find it easier to spot these thoughts whenever they arise. This may allow us to rest more easily.

For those who are struggling a lot against the practice of resting in presence, the Inquiries can be helpful. Support and guidance from others are also beneficial. It can be worthwhile to start a mentoring relationship with a servant (see Appendix) who has direct experience with overcoming this kind of struggle.

Some who come to this way of recovery may believe they're excluded from presence, or that resting in presence is impossible for them. These are just temporary viewpoints coming and going within presence. They seem true only if we repeatedly emphasize them. No one is excluded from presence.

We take it easy on ourselves, letting the practice of presence unfold in its own way. We're not in a race toward the future. We're not in a race against others. We're simply becoming comfortable with the present moment in exactly the way it's appearing for us, even if its current appearance includes viewpoints about the difficulty of resting in presence.

Misconceptions About Deep Rest

Some may never experience a period in which thought stops or slows down substantially. This is fine. The cessation of thought isn't necessary.

For these people, there may be no need to experience long periods of not thinking. They come to experience quietness and rest as underlying and permeating the movement of all energies. Thoughts either arise or they don't. Either way, there's no identification with them.

Others may experience a period in which thought substantially quiets. We call this *deep rest*.

A deep rest period is a phase in which many concepts just stop appearing. The mind feels almost totally at rest. This deep rest may help some of us to disidentify from certain tightly held thoughts or beliefs that make up the core of the self-center. A deep rest period, however, isn't a requirement of this method.

In presence, we are truly at rest, whether thoughts and emotions are arising or not.

Through resting in presence, we find we no longer identify with thought and other temporary energies. That doesn't mean that thoughts must stop appearing.

In no longer identifying with thought (regardless of how that happens), we're freed from the cycle of addictive seeking.

Whether or not we experience a deep rest period, concepts that were once thought to be real may no longer appear real or true anymore. As we identify less with thought, the world may take on a dreamlike or unreal quality.

We want to be aware of any extreme viewpoints that may arise when identification with thought falls away. For example, there may be a tendency to emphasize such thoughts as *There's no path to presence, Nothing exists,* or *All viewpoints are false.*

These are also just viewpoints. There's nothing wrong with any viewpoint. But the freedom available here comes from restful presence, which is the space in which all viewpoints appear and disappear. The freedom doesn't come from emphasizing really spiritual-sounding ideas or extreme viewpoints.

All ideas are seen to be equal energies. This is good news. We come to see that no thought we emphasize can bring us closer to presence—and no thought can take us away from presence.

Each thought is seen to be like a breeze blowing through the air. It has no power to displace the air itself.

Those who do experience a deep rest period or disidentification from thought may experience confusion and frustration as one's personal motivation around certain issues begins to fall away. The personal viewpoints and other things that once motivated us to seek the future start to drop. This is fine! The self-center is being seen through. This is a normal phase that some people go through.

The confusion and frustration come from the last remnants of the addictive seeker, who is still looking for something else to happen. The old mechanism of personal seeking is still faintly operating. It appears in the form of subtle frustration in not knowing what to do next. It's often accompanied by a little voice that asks, "What's next?" This voice is still the addict talking. It's the seeker.

As our self-centered story is seen through and as our seeking toward future stops, selfless presence takes over. Selfless presence is realized when the voice asking "What's next?" falls away or is no longer being emphasized.

In selfless presence, we have no idea how life is going to unfold. We have no interest in the question "What's next?" We see the personal demand behind the question. We see that the question implies we're supposed to be in control or know what happens. With every demand on life, resistance is operating. When there's resistance to life, there's seeking toward the future for release.

When we resist what happens and try to control outcomes, we work against life. When we live in not knowing, having no personal demand on how things must unfold, life works through us.

Selfless presence is complete openness. In selfless presence, we aren't demanding that something else needs to happen. We live with open arms. A simple love of life resides in our hearts.

We remain open to whatever's happening and to whatever way life is actually unfolding. This is complete acceptance and surrender.

It's freedom from the addictive cycle of seeking. It's the beginning of living life in a totally new way. (See chapter 9, "Freedom.")

In deep rest, we aren't trying to get rid of thought permanently. The benefit of deep rest is only to disidentify from thought, not to kill the mind. It's not meant to help you escape life or the world. The mind continues to have a practical function in our lives, no matter how deeply we've realized that our real identity doesn't reside in thought.

Another trap that some people report during a deep rest period is detachment, or even nihilism.

In deep rest, we want to notice any viewpoints that lead us to feel detached from what's happening, from life and other people.

Enjoying moments of quiet solitude is fine and can help us experience restful presence. But detaching from others is unhealthy. It arises as a result of a negative viewpoint or emotional resistance toward life, others, or the world. Detachment isn't selfless presence. It's another form of separation.

Deep rest is not "depressed." Depression comes from tuning out of our present, immediate experience and isolating back into the world of thoughts. It is a lack of intimacy with what is, a strategy of avoidance. Depression arises from emphasizing negative stories and not letting all emotions be as they are. Deep rest is a quiet mind that does not *identify* with thoughts and emotions as they pass through. In deep rest, anything and everything can arise, but we find no sense of self in anything that arises. This frees us to live fully but without our thoughts and emotions taking up our entire attention.

Through resting in presence, we come to see that we cannot truly separate ourselves from our present experience. And our present experience is life itself. Therefore, when we're buying into thoughts of detachment, we're buying into a false sense of separation between self and other, or self and life. We're hiding or trying to escape having to feel pain that may arise in relationships.

In noticing any thoughts of detachment, and resting in presence, we're already free of these thoughts of separation. In restful, thought-free presence, we're awake to the emotional resistance that's driving these viewpoints. In letting those emotional energies be as they are, the need to detach releases itself. We feel more and more comfortable in relationship.

Facing the suffering and conflict in relationship is precisely how we wake up from overreliance on divisive viewpoints and identification with the self-center. Relationship is not something to avoid. It's a vehicle through which we realize freedom.

We rest in alert, awake presence, welcoming our present situation as it is. Our communications with others are vibrantly alive, not deadened or pushed away in favor of silence. We're listening, living, and loving—not escaping into silence in order to avoid conflict or painful feelings. The quietness of presence is an opening, not a closing. It opens us to everything that's happening within and around us. If we begin to use presence as a way to close ourselves off, this is a sign that detachment is happening.

Nihilism is an extreme form of detachment that can arise, although it's rare. Nihilism is the belief that there's no meaning or purpose in life.

Don't mistake nihilism for spiritual awakening or presence. Nihilism is a belief system. If we experience nihilism, it means we're emphasizing thoughts about life being without purpose or meaning. These are viewpoints based on a resistance to life. In noticing them as nothing more than viewpoints, we can be free of them.

Presence isn't about detaching from life or the world. It's not about living in a story that life is meaningless. It's about disidentifying from thought, emotion, and other energies that arise and fall. This happens automatically and effortlessly through resting in presence.

Detachment and disidentification are two totally different things. We don't want to confuse them. Let's revisit the pond metaphor from chapter 1 to explain the difference.

Restful, selfless presence is like the pond. The energies that come and go within presence are the same as ripples across the pond's surface. The pond and the ripples are inseparable. The ripples are all the thoughts, emotions, sensations, people, situations, and relationships that come and go within presence. To deny life in all its diverse appearances is to deny presence itself.

Trying to push away these energies is like a pond trying to push away its own ripples.

Detachment happens when we take a negative attitude toward the ripples. We try to keep from experiencing the world of ripples, pushing them all away. This comes from personal will. *In detachment, we're at war with what is.*

In *disidentification*, we carry no resistance toward the ripples. As the pond, we allow each ripple to be as it is. We see that each ripple is temporary. So no ripple can define or move the pond.

Whereas detachment carries negative feelings of loneliness, sadness, or apathy, disidentification reveals a natural peace, freedom, well-being, and equanimity available in every moment.

Presence is the realization that we're inseparable from life, from others, and from whatever's happening in life.

Presence is love, not detachment.

Mistaking Presence for Stagnancy

If we emphasize viewpoints about presence rather than experientially resting in presence, we may imagine that presence is about stagnancy. This is another misconception about presence. *Stagnancy* is a state of not developing, flowing, or changing.

Again, the pond metaphor is helpful here. Presence is like the deep, still pond that's always changelessly at rest. We rely on this presence completely. It provides unshakable mental and emotional stability. In this rest, we find freedom from the cycle of addictive seeking.

But this stability isn't stagnancy. In presence, we're not stuck in a state where nothing happens or where we oppose change. Life continues happening. The ripples continue flowing across the surface of the pond and are seen to be inseparable from the pond.

Life contains a radical diversity of energies, including thoughts, emotions, states, sensations, experiences, people, relationships, perspectives, families, and careers. We come to see these as temporary, illusive movements within presence.

In this way of recovery, we're not disengaging or denying this fluid flow of diversity and change. This flow has no independent existence from presence. We embrace life fully. We see ourselves as life itself appearing as this perfect flow of diverse energies.

We experience a deepening in presence. As more and more self-centered viewpoints are seen through, a deeper surrender is available. This deepening isn't the self-center engaged in its usual game of personal seeking. Seeking comes from emphasizing thoughts about the future; it's based in a present sense of lack.

Deepening is different. It comes from seeing through those viewpoints and being able to relax effortlessly into the natural rest of the present moment. Deepening is a movement of selflessness. It opens us up more and more to the natural abundance within us and all around us, and to the completeness of the present moment.

In the present moment, life unfolds in a mysterious way. We never know what's going to happen next. We simply remain open to the constantly changing energies flowing within presence.

In selfless presence, we may still achieve, grow, learn, and evolve over time. We may still explore new opportunities, advance in our jobs, and be successful in the world, if that's what appeals to us. Presence doesn't outlaw anything. Presence is an opening, not a closing.

The difference is there's no personal seeking behind these movements. The present moment remains primary, always.

In presence, we aren't looking to the future for personal fulfillment. So we're able to be fully here in the present moment. It leaves us open to explore the unfolding of life without personal expectations. In no longer looking to the future for personal fulfillment, we may even continue to have goals, but they are held more lightly, without an attachment to any particular outcome or course of action. We're content no matter how life unfolds within this present space.

Selfless presence leaves us open to create in the world, in a whole new way.

We open ourselves up to possibilities that aren't available whenever we're operating from a self-centered story of lack.

When we live from lack, we only want to take. Our creative energy is stifled. We're always seeking personal gain. This narrows our vision. We look at the world with self-centered tunnel vision. We live in a cycle of personal seeking toward the future.

Selfless presence is abundance. When we live in abundance, we seek nothing for ourselves. We experience contentment simply for being alive. We only want to give and be open to whatever unfolds in the next moment. We're truly open to positive change, for others, the world, and ourselves. Yet, we remain unattached to outcomes.

Making Presence into a Thing

Reading words like "presence" so often in this book, or other words like "natural rest," can lead to making words into things. The mind thinks only in terms of objects. So it is natural that it would think of presence as a thing. This can lead to dogmatic thinking, in which presence is defended or treated like a religion. Be careful of this tendency. The easiest way to see that presence is not a thing the mind can grasp is to use the UI. Try to find presence. Is the word "presence" it? No, that's just a word. How about that peaceful feeling or sensation you feel—is that it? No, that is a feeling or something you sense. Keep looking… Presence is as unfindable as any object you try to find using the UI. Do yourself a favor and use the UI on any word on which you find yourself stuck. Be free of all dogmatic thinking. That kind of deep freedom cannot be realized by hanging on to such concepts.

Key Points

The following are the most important points to remember from this chapter:

Spotting traps and misconceptions. Come back to chapter 8 after you have practiced the tools in this book for a while. Notice whether any of the traps or misconceptions in this chapter are arising for you.

Get help. If you notice any traps or misconceptions arising, seek help from a facilitator or talk to people in Natural Rest groups, which are discussed in the appendix. Getting support from others is critical in overcoming these traps and misconceptions. It is sometimes difficult to spot these traps and misconceptions within ourselves. Hearing others share in Natural Rest groups can help us spot and deal with these issues.

CHAPTER 9

Freedom

The natural rest of presence has obvious benefits. The words in this chapter are not intended as dangling carrots that pull us into more seeking toward the future. These benefits are realized through the recognition of timeless, selfless freedom. As described in the last chapter, the benefits arise from *deepening into this present recognition*, not seeking some later point in your time-bound story.

In this deepening, we see through the self-center, which is the time-bound story.

Selflessness reveals itself naturally in this recognition.

In this selflessness, we're no longer attached to images within the story of self. We're free of attachment to the past as well as the future. We're no longer attached to the identity of being a separate person, totally cut off from others and the world.

The memory of our past is still available. The future continues to unfold. But our sense of identity is no longer found in thoughts of the past or future.

We live in simple, timeless being.

The present moment remains primary in all situations. We find that acceptance and surrender aren't things that we *do*. Rather, they're natural attributes available in presence.

We're no longer guided by guilt, sadness, depression, or anxiety. We no longer believe that we're a conceptual label. No label from the past sticks at this point, including the label "addict" or even "recovering addict."

Self-centered thoughts may still arise, but we're no longer identified with them.

Thoughts, emotions, cravings, states, and sensations that once remained unseen, and that once fueled our seeking, are now seen. They no longer have power over us.

We experience life as a seamless flow. A moment of rest feels seamlessly inseparable from a movement of energy, and vice versa.

All energies are seen to be inseparable and equal appearances of presence.

We find a seamless balance between all energies.

We feel at home in the present moment and experience equanimity and well-being regardless of what else is happening.

We see through the dualism of the mind. We no longer find ourselves attached to one side of a pair of opposites—like right versus wrong, positive versus negative, or black versus white. We're open to seeing and embracing each side.

We find that thought still arises, but it's experienced as lighter, more transparent, quieter, more in the background, and much less personal than it was in our seeking days.

As thought feels less personal, the sense of separation between self and other people and things relaxes. We respect conventional boundaries, but we live in a loving, compassionate, and undivided way in *all* relationships.

We welcome all viewpoints as they appear. Thought is allowed to come and go, without ever forming a separate self.

Emotions have no ability to torture us anymore. They come and they go. They leave no trace.

Each thought, emotion, craving, sensation, state, and experience comes and goes effortlessly, spontaneously, and causelessly.

Each movement is uninterruptedly allowed to arise and fall. Each movement of energy disappears into the still, quiet space of presence.

The personal will that was trying to control all that energy falls away.

Selfless presence stops looking less like a practice and more like what we are, in the most basic sense.

Life lives itself through us.

We realize fully that we don't know what's going to happen next. This *not knowing* provides unconditional freedom. We see that we *never* knew what was going to happen, even in the days of personal seeking when we used to be attached to outcomes. We were living a lie!

We effortlessly allow everything to be as it is. We allow the future to unfold without trying to control how it unfolds.

We lose the desire to use addictive substances and engage in addictive activities. We know that the only reason we were using these substances and activities in our seeking days is because we were looking for our freedom.

Selfless presence contains a natural well-being and freedom that no drug or other addictive substance can ever bring. This is why we're free of the need to relapse.

Drugs and addictive activities are poor substitutes for the well-being and freedom of presence.

Cravings all but disappear. And if they appear, they have no charge. Without a charge, they disappear, leaving no trace.

Obsession loses its control over us. It greatly diminishes or stops arising altogether. If obsession appears, it's noticed immediately. We see that it arises in a presence that allows it to be completely as it is. In this awareness, obsession loses its ability to continue.

In presence, our contentment, freedom, and peace are uncaused and unconditional. We no longer believe that other people and things hold the key to our contentment, freedom, or peace.

We no longer believe that seeking something else in the future is necessary for contentment. No temporary substance or activity can add to a timeless freedom and well-being that's total and complete as it is.

We're free to experience this moment with fresh eyes and ears and with a heart fully open to each experience, each person, each viewpoint.

We're unafraid of and unattached to outcomes. Without expectations, every moment is a gift—a welcomed guest, perfect just as it is.

By "perfect," we don't mean that conflicts no longer arise or that challenging situations like divorce, unemployment, physical pain, illness, and death don't occur. These things may occur.

"Perfect," in this sense, means that presence provides a natural and limitless capacity to fully face, but not identify with, the thoughts and emotions that appear in these situations. Even during challenging times, we experience an undercurrent of well-being.

This well-being permeates every moment. We no longer seek to alter our moods with addictive substances or activities. We no longer chase after pleasant feelings in avoidance of pain that may arise in challenging situations.

We no longer need an outside fix. We have inner peace, contentment, and freedom.

In selfless presence, we realize a naturally occurring gratitude that's present simply because we're alive. This gratitude isn't tied to things we acquire or to what we hope might happen in the future. It isn't dependent on circumstances or situations.

In selfless presence, we notice the simple wonders of life that escaped us when we were trapped in constant seeking toward the future.

We notice the feel of a breeze on our faces, the sound of traffic, a bird singing outside our window, the voice of a friend and his story, or the sheer gratitude for simply breathing and being alive.

We enjoy the simplicity of whatever's appearing *in this moment*.

We find that life is and was always here, in the present moment, waiting for us to discover it beyond our self-centered, time-bound stories.

No longer identifying with our self-centered story doesn't mean that presence erases individuality.

We retain our individual talents, skills, knowledge, and other unique attributes. We find that we each bring something unique to relationships and to life. We cherish this uniqueness.

In seeing through the self-center, we no longer use these attributes for selfish gain, or as a way to feel better or more special than others.

We utilize these attributes in a selfless way for the benefit of everyone. This takes no effort, planning, control, or manipulation. It happens naturally and effortlessly through the simple recognition of presence.

In selfless presence, we find no need for hope. We see that hope was based only on seeking.

Hope is based on the idea that the present moment lacks something and that this lack will be filled in the future. In selfless presence, there's no lack, so there's no longer a need for hope.

In recognizing selflessness, the personal search for something more ends. We discover an uncontrived, unconditional presence that isn't dependent on any experience and yet permeates every experience.

Presence lacks nothing, so the search for something more in the future naturally falls away. Yet we remain completely open to learning and to life's constant unfolding.

We see that the viewpoints "I have arrived at spiritual awakening" and "I have not arrived yet" are equal energies of presence. We don't have to emphasize either viewpoint for a sense of self. We simply live as what we really are—presence.

We remain open to taking multiple perspectives and to seeing where we may get stuck in a particular viewpoint that separates us from others. In seeing where we're stuck, we awaken again to the possibility of remaining completely open, compassionate, and loving.

Each moment is its own awakening.

In taking the perspectives of others, we're better able to see life from the viewpoints of our sons, daughters, spouses, partners, coworkers, bosses, family members, and people from other political parties, religions, philosophies, or countries.

This creates compassion and harmony. It heals any damaged relationships from our past.

We expect nothing in return for our actions in our relationships. No longer do we take action in order to receive a personal benefit.

We no longer expect people to do or say what we want them to do or say. Each person who comes within our presence is allowed to be exactly as he or she is.

Each moment is accepted exactly as it is.

When we remain open to the present moment in this way, we find our calling in life.

At a minimum, we operate in each moment in natural, selfless, timeless acceptance. When we're engaged in projects that excite us, we experience a vibrant, alive inspiration and enthusiasm.

As the addictive seeking energy dissolves through this way of recovery, all that's left is our natural energy. It becomes freely available to us in the here and now.

Life's no longer a chore. It's a gift.

In selflessness, the question "What benefits everyone?" becomes an aspect of our very being. Wisdom and compassion arise naturally in each situation. We live to be of service.

Being of service comes naturally and effortlessly in selflessness. It never feels like work.

In selflessness, love takes action through us. Love is recognizing itself everywhere, in every person we encounter.

When the self-center falls away, we want to help others.

We find ourselves wanting to be engaged in our communities. We get involved with causes that benefit others. This happens naturally, as a result of no longer being self-centered.

Selfless presence includes being fully engaged with life. It's seeing that we are life itself, aware of itself, and taking care of itself...in every area.

We experience life as an unchanging, stable, selfless presence in which the dynamic flow of change naturally occurs.

Each moment is experienced as completely fresh, revealing that whatever arises is only temporary. It is not who we are. The past and future no longer rule our experience. Emotional pain becomes the way into freedom instead of something to escape.

Addiction is no longer seen as a death sentence or even a life sentence. It becomes the doorway to present freedom through rest and inquiry.

Recovery never has to be about seeking the future again. It's always about seeing that this moment lacks nothing and that there is nothing to seek. In this moment-by-moment seeing, we remain open to look into any self-centered stories that may pop up from time to time and to undo any Velcro Effect with the Living Inquiries. That's not seeking. That's present looking.

Always keep recovery simple: *Rest* in the midst of whatever is happening. *Inquire* when needed. And *enjoy life!*

Acknowledgments

Special thanks to my teachers: Eckhart Tolle, Adyashanti, Candice O'Denver, and Greg Goode. Special thanks to the following: New Harbinger Publications, Chad for his undying love and support, Mom, Dad, Mark, Teri, Kevin, Jolinda Kirby, preliminary editors Z and Scotty Rathjen, editor C. J. Schepers for her amazing editing touch, Curt King for all his work above and beyond the call of duty, Bart McFarlane for his devotion and attention to all things related to Natural Rest and for editing that really enhanced the book, Jeff Foster for his support, my friends from the NA fellowship for helping me in the beginning of recovery, and David Langer and John Raatz for their help and creativity in the beginning. Special thanks to Colette Kelso for codeveloping the Compulsion Inquiry with me and to Colette and Fiona Robertson for developing the Anxiety Inquiry. Thanks to the Living Inquiries senior facilitators and trainers for their devoted attention to the further development of the Inquiries. No act is done alone. No man or woman is an island unto himself or herself. Without the support of these people and so many others, this book would never have made it into the hands of a single reader. These are the people who have graciously and selflessly given me the support and space I needed to write this book. Thank you, from the deepest place in my heart!

Resources

Scott Kiloby's Websites

Scott's website containing information relevant to addiction and recovery: http://www.naturalrestforaddiction.com

For information about participation at the Kiloby Center for Recovery: http://www.kilobycenter.com

Scott's main site: http://www.kiloby.com

For more information about the Living Inquiries: http://www.livinginquiries.com

Appendix

Natural Rest Groups

Natural Rest groups can be a powerful mechanism for mutual support in recovery. Mutual support of each other, especially in the beginning of recovery, is beneficial.

Some people may not feel comfortable being involved with a group. They may choose to work on their own. This isn't recommended. If this is your choice, it's suggested that you find support with at least one other person involved with this way of recovery.

Natural Rest group meetings may take place online or in a local community. A meeting is any gathering of two or more who come together for the purpose of supporting one another in this way of recovery.

This appendix is meant only as a general guideline or set of suggestions. Natural Rest groups have autonomy. They govern themselves.

Groups may take donations during meetings in order to be fully self-supporting and to pay rent for the facility in which the meeting takes place, as well as any other costs associated with meetings.

Natural Rest groups and meetings should center on the practices in this book. They should provide those attending with information on how to find this book and any other online or written literature on this topic.

Natural Rest is a participatory way of recovery that values involvement at a group level, including the importance of relationship, mutual support, equality, diversity, dialogue, and inclusiveness. All voices are welcome in Natural Rest meetings. In this book, the "we" pronoun is used to designate the importance of relationships and mutual support in recovery.

Mutual support and participation at the group level is beneficial for addicts. Simply being around others who are discovering the benefit of presence is contagious. Mutual support and participation also help us avoid isolation. Isolation can lead to loneliness, depression, and even relapse.

With Natural Rest group meetings, our intent is to form safe places, both online and in our local communities, for those who are ready to find recovery through presence.

These meetings are places where people can share their experiences and ask for the guidance of those who have a more direct experience of the natural rest of the present moment.

This book uses simple language in order to reach as many people as possible. The language is also designed to avoid conflict between varying belief systems, religions, philosophies, and worldviews.

All belief systems, religions, philosophies, and worldviews are absolutely welcome here. But we also ask that no one impose his or her viewpoint on another. No mental viewpoint is absolutized here.

To absolutize (dictate) a viewpoint is to characterize it as absolute truth and mentally emphasize it above all others. This can only lead to a rigid sense of separation between us. When we separate ourselves from one another by absolutizing or dictating a viewpoint, we lose sight of what this way of recovery is really about—finding recovery through presence. Mutual support works best when we release the idea of being right and focus instead on being of service to each other.

Any insights gained through resting are valuable. Insights open us up to resting more fully. We share our insights as a service to others, whenever such service is requested. We *don't* impose our viewpoints on others. We see that insights and viewpoints can be helpful, but they're poor substitutes for experientially resting in presence.

In these meetings, our only interest is mutually supporting each other to realize the natural benefits of resting in presence.

Forming or Finding a Natural Rest Group

You may find an already established group of people in your area who have joined together to help each other with this way of recovery from addiction. This is called a Natural Rest group. You may form a group in your area if one is not established already.

Visit http://www.naturalrestforaddiction.com to find or establish a Natural Rest group in your area.

Servants

If Natural Rest groups are formed, they should contain elected "servants" who help to conduct the meetings and take care of the administrative needs of the group. Servants should be people who have direct experience with the benefit of presence as it pertains to recovery. They should be available in meetings to answer questions and give gentle guidance to those who are new to the program.

Those who are new to Natural Rest may want to find a servant to act as a mentor. In order to be a servant who mentors another, a person should have direct experience with the benefits of restful presence as well as the other tools in this book.

Servants should, at all times, refrain from imposing their viewpoints on others. To be a servant is to be of service to others, not to teach or preach to others.

Being a servant isn't about being special in the eyes of others.

A servant's function is to serve with selflessness, honesty, integrity, compassion, and humility, without a desire for attention, praise, or acknowledgment. This selflessness, of course, is naturally available in presence.

A servant never seeks a return on his or her investment in any relationship. He or she gives without the expectation of any particular result.

Natural Rest groups may also designate servants with specific skills to run meetings, take care of group money, and perform other administrative duties. Servants aren't in charge of the group. They have no authority. The group as a whole has the authority. All actions should be taken from the perspective of what's beneficial for everyone involved.

Servants may also act as mentors in one-on-one relationships. Those who are new to this way of recovery may need direct guidance and help in the beginning. They can request a servant to act as a mentor.

Servants can share their direct experience with resting in presence and help with inquiries and the other tools from this book.

The function of these relationships isn't to identify with roles such as newcomer, servant, and mentor. We're not any of these conceptual labels. These relationships serve to support us as we directly experience the benefits of restful presence.

Servants may have experience facilitating the Compulsion, Unfindable, and Anxiety Inquiries or the Boomerang. But servants are not necessarily formally trained as facilitators.

There are people available who are formally trained as facilitators and who work over the phone and the Internet with others. See http://www.livinginquiries.com.

Anonymity and Confidentiality

We never share the names of those participating in meetings with anyone outside the group. Whatever's shared within a meeting by anyone is considered confidential.

This confidentiality and privacy is necessary to provide a safe place where people can feel comfortable enough to be open and honest about their experience and to request guidance without fearing negative ramifications in their careers or any area of their lives.

Scott Kiloby is a noted author, teacher, and international speaker on non-duality and mindfulness as it applies to addiction, depression, anxiety, and trauma. As someone who lived in the addictive cycle for over twenty years, he's made the journey to freedom from addiction himself, discovering and refining the insights and methods presented in this book along the way. Kiloby is founder of a worldwide community of Living Inquiries facilitators who work with people in over twelve different countries, and cofounder and CEO of The Kiloby Center for Recovery in Rancho Mirage, CA, the first addiction, anxiety, trauma, and depression treatment center to focus primarily on mindfulness. He is co-owner of the Natural Rest House, a detox and residential center in the Palm Springs, CA, area. Kiloby is also COO of MyLife Recovery Centers, an addiction treatment program that provides the innovative Naltrexone Implant, which greatly reduces or eliminates cravings for opiates and alcohol for several months. He is currently developing intensive outpatient programs for MyLife across the United States, in which his mindfulness work will be provided to patients who receive the implant.

Foreword writer **Jeff Foster** studied astrophysics at Cambridge University. He holds meetings, retreats, and private sessions around the world, gently but directly pointing people back to the deep acceptance inherent in the present moment. He was voted #51 in *Watkins Mind Body Spirit*'s 2012 list of the world's 100 Most Spiritually Influential Living People. His website is www.lifewithoutacentre.com.

MORE BOOKS from NON-DUALITY PRESS

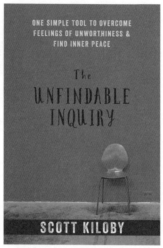

ISBN: 978-1626258129 | US $16.95

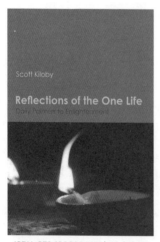

ISBN: 978-1908664471 | US $19.95

ISBN: 978-1908664464 | US $13.95

NON-DUALITY PRESS
An Imprint of New Harbinger Publications
www.newharbinger.com